CU00703763

RACE WARRIORS

The Perverse Results of Anti-Racism

Russell Lewis is a veteran commentator on politics, having been for many years a leader and feature-writer, first on the *Daily* and *Sunday Telegraph* and then on the *Daily Mail*. He is the author of numerous books and pamphlets, including a best-selling biography of Margaret Thatcher. In a varied career he has been Chairman of the Bow Group, Head of the European Community Press Office in London, Director of the Conservative Political Centre, General Director of the Institute of Economic Affairs, and Director of the Maastricht Referendum Campaign and of the European Foundation.

Also by Russell Lewis

Rome or Brussels
The New Service Society
The Reactionary Joke Book (with Christie Davies)
Margaret Thatcher: A Political and Personal Biography
The Survival of Capitalism
Tony Benn
The Official Shop Steward's Joke Book
A Memoir of F C Scott
The Deadwright State
Several Bruges Group pamphlets

RACE WARRIORS

The Perverse Results of Anti-Racism

Russell Lewis

with a Foreword by
Narindar Saroop, CBE

NEW EUROPEAN PUBLICATIONS LTD

Published in the United Kingdom in 2003 by

New European Publications Limited
14-16 Carroun Road
London SW8 1JT, England

All rights reserved. No part of this publication may be repro-
duced, stored in a retrieval system, or transmitted, in any form or
by any means, electronic, mechanical, photocopying, recording
or otherwise, without the prior permission of New European
Publications Limited.

This book is sold subject to the condition that it shall not, by
way of trade or otherwise, be lent, re-sold, hired out or otherwise
circulated without the publisher's prior consent in any form of
binding or cover other than that in which it is published and without a similar condition including this condition being imposed
upon the subsequent purchaser.

British Library Cataloguing in Publication Data
ISBN 1-872410-30-8

Copyright © Russell Lewis

Typesetting by KAD

Printed and bound in Great Britain by CLE Print, St Ives

Contents

Acknowledgements

I should like to express my gratitude to the following for advice, material and ideas for this book: Professors Christie Davies and Antony Flew of Reading University; Digby Anderson; Christine Chapman of BBC Television; Peter Burden and Anthony Doran, of the *Daily Mail*. Derek Hill; Ronald Spark; Stuart Butler, Director of Domestic Policy Studies at the Heritage Foundation, Washington, and my ever-helpful former colleagues in the *Daily Mail* library.

I am also grateful to the following for comments: Lord Monson and Sir Richard Body. I should especially like to thank Dr Barry Bracewell-Milns for his help and support in editing and getting the final text into publishable shape.

Russell Lewis

Foreword

by

Narindar Saroop CBE

In the mid-1970s, when I was adopted as a parliamentary candidate, the media inevitably labelled me as an Asian. Equally inevitably I was propelled into the front line of the issues of Immigration and Race Relations, notwithstanding repeated declarations on my part that I was just another Parliamentary candidate whose primary interests were Defence and Foreign Affairs. In one television interview, Sir Robin Day asked my opinion about how prevalent was colour prejudice, and he criticised me for being enigmatic when I replied, "Less than is imagined, but more than can be identified". It has ever been thus. Prejudice of all kinds, including colour, is endemic in human behaviour and nature, and is felt and practised throughout the world. Any prejudice is demeaning and hurtful for those at its receiving end. The spoken word can be cruel, even more sometimes than other forms of prejudice, although it need not always be so. There was once a light-heartedness and humour, with no malice, as for example in various terms that the British and Indian troops had for each other when they were comrades in arms. In no way was this meant or taken as derogatory. Over a number of years, some of my friends have addressed me as 'wog', a term for them and myself of affection and endearment, and they would turn ferociously on anyone else who might feel himself or herself presuming to use the same word. These days all this would be categorised as serious racial abuse. Stories about the Scotsman the Irishman, the Indian, etc., are now not tolerated, and our overall humour is the poorer for it.

I was also asked at that time about how I viewed the future. The balance sheet showed that the credit side of the Asian community was their hard work, family cohesion and thrift. The debit side was their lack of communication in English. The future two decades would remove the linguistic disadvantage, with the second generation fluent in their local Southall or Bradford patois, and one could envisage a proliferation of millionaires and creation of employment beyond that foreseen initially. The Afro-Caribbean community had little language difficulty, and their first generation felt some sentiment for "The Mother Country", which all hoped would continue.

I was right and wrong, but such of my hopes as have not been borne out have not diluted my optimism. Although the family cohesion has diminished, compact communities pursue more or less their own way of life within the overall network. It is assimilation or integration of a different kind. It is remarkable how a small country has absorbed the large numbers involved. There has been no widespread upheaval or civil strife, and to the credit of the white community, the vast majority of the new Britons have quietly and successfully melted away into their local areas, contributing skills and wealth, and beginning to be involved in civic and public affairs. I would hope that a number of them would articulate the debt they owe to this country, which provided shelter and opportunity. They should point out that it is in their interest to support our institutions, viz.: the Monarchy, Parliament, the Judiciary and the Armed Forces. I have not forgotten the Church, but there are many well-supported "churches". It should be remembered that whenever a country is weak, internally or externally, its ethnic minorities are likely to be the first to suffer. It is in their self-interest to say: "I am proud to be British". Part of the greatness of Great Britain lies in its ability to accept, nurture and assimilate those who are strangers yesterday, but are part of its fabric today.

On balance, the Race Relations legislation was well-intended and the right thing to implement, in order to combat some deplorable discrimination in the workplace and the social sphere. But like many other good intentions, it is the implementation that gives cause for concern. In some instances, it has been used as a sledgehammer to crack a nut. God or nature, depending on your belief, provides a rich diversity, and homogeneity palls, truth that we all know but agree not to talk about. Within a framework of fairness for all, society is healthier by ignoring social scientists who will not tolerate perceived differences in the strengths and weaknesses of various races.

I have known Russell Lewis for around twenty years, during which his stance against racism has been clear. It is gratifying that his research and work in outlining how and where the fight against racism is going wrong is now published.

Narindar Saroop

1

Not a Happy Tale

These introductory remarks are written in the shadow of the attack on the World Trade Center in New York, the worst racist atrocity of the 21st century. It has been projected as an assault on the heart of the global capitalist system, which indeed it was, but the Islamic terrorists responsible were undoubtedly conscious of another potent symbolism of this criminal act — that they were also delivering a blow at the most Jewish American city ("War to the Death between America and Islamic terrorists" by Daniel Johnson, *Daily Telegraph* 12.9.2001). Indeed, as racists, the Arabic fundamentalists have few rivals. It is therefore bizarre, to say the least, that this shameful event followed hard on the heels of the United Nations Conference on Racism in Durban, South Africa. The inspiration, or anyway chief support, for this egregious exercise came from the Arab states, which sought to turn it into an anti-Zionist fest. In fact they failed to get adopted their original wording of a motion branding Israel a racist and apartheid state; but even the amended version describing Israel as an occupying power was too much for the Israeli and the US representatives, who walked out. Of course I am not equating all the Arab states with the racism and inhumanity which motivated the terrorists who demolished the twin towers in New York. It is clear that the majority of Moslems condemn this barbarous act. That is also true of most Moslem governments. What I am suggesting is that the Arab rulers, who usually take a sensible view of international affairs where Israel is not involved, have been tempted into using the vocabulary of the professional anti-racists as a convenient way of anathematising the Israelis and gaining popular support. For the governments in these Middle-Eastern states generally lack democratic legitimacy, look for their subjects' approval by denouncing Israel and have played the dangerous game of financing extremist groups basically hostile to themselves. So, at Durban, they backed demands that western countries should pay compensation for the slavery of Africans and for the sins of colonialism in times past. They ignored the role of many African agents who rounded up and sold their compatriots into slavery. They also overlooked the long and much more prolonged record of Arab slavery. As for the colonialist charge, as Mark Steyn of the *Spectator* remarked, the emerging nations have suffered more from independence than colonialism. In this context it is worth noting that far more lives were lost in the civil war in Biafra, Nigeria, than in all the colonial wars in British history.

All of which highlights the reality that though, broadly speaking, since the first edition appeared the evils of racism have waned ("Racist attitudes may still be widespread, but in fewer places do they determine an individual's life chances" — *The Economist*, commenting on the Durban conference, 1.9.2001), the influence and clout of the self-styled anti-racists have waxed. Meanwhile the associated humbug has reached new highs.

My original theme

The Essential Argument

The core message of my comments published fifteen years ago is still the same today, but its urgency is greater. It was that the worthy and widespread desire to combat the evil of racism in our society has been wantonly misdirected by the race relations lobby and the Commission for Racial

Equality, which has acted as its poodle. Policies have been adopted which, for all the spin put on their presentation, have promoted not racial harmony but discord. Worse, what can properly be called the race relations industry — and a nationalised industry at that, since it is almost wholly dependent on public funding — has embraced an agenda which reaches far beyond the promotion of racial harmony, which should be its raison d'etre, but in which its role has been counterproductive. Instead its members have exploited the universal abhorrence of the racist crimes of Hitler's National Socialism to justify and implement a latter-day witch-hunt, which threatens to subvert the very roots of our democratic ethos and sense of justice.

Made in USA

As I pointed out then, the inspiration of these policies has come from America and that is just what is wrong with them. For, on this issue, America has been a model to avoid. Indeed, it is astounding how ignorant these would-be imitators have been of the resounding failure of the race policy experiments on the other side of the Atlantic. There is no need to dwell at length here on the ruthless exposure by Charles Murray of the catastrophic results of Lyndon B. Johnson's anti-poverty programme (primarily aimed at the black poor) in promoting welfare dependency in whole swathes of the population. Nor to underline the equally damning critiques of American exercises in affirmative action by distinguished black American economists like Thomas Sowell and Walter Williams. These are fully chronicled in the original text. I will content myself with pointing again to one striking observation by Sowell about his country's experience. This is that America's economically most successful ethnic groups, namely the Japanese and the Chinese, have deliberately eschewed politics as a means of improving their condition, despite grave past injustices, and have relied entirely on their own efforts. By contrast the indigenous Indians, who have campaigned for and won huge welfare handouts and many exclusive privileges as compensation for historic wrongs, are the least-favoured ethnic group in the whole population by every relevant measure of human welfare. More generally, decades of reverse race discrimination policies, far from healing ethnic divisions, have polarised American society.

Race Awareness

I further pointed to the damage done to race relations in this country by the policies, which the Commission for Racial Equality (CRE) and its cohorts have favoured. Particularly pernicious has been its campaign to increase race awareness among various groups of the host population. For commonsense would suggest that reducing consciousness of race differences, indeed cultivating colour blindness, should be the prime objective. During officially-prescribed race relations courses perfectly normal individuals have been humiliated and obliged to confess to racist feelings, often under pain, if they object, of loss of employment, promotion, or pension. Such schemes are an odious exercise in thought control and persecution of those whose attitudes are not politically correct and could hardly be better designed to provoke and magnify the very racist feelings they are supposed to suppress. Such procedures are uncomfortably reminiscent of the brainwashing techniques used by the Maoist Chinese on British prisoners during the Korean War.

Quota Craze

I also warned of another, perverse approach of the Commission for Racial Equality towards allegedly improving the social and economic condition of the ethnic

minorities. This was through the promotion and imposition
of quotas — according to the false doctrine that equality
of opportunity is reflected in equality of result. By this
rubric, the ethnics' share of jobs, status, wealth, schooling,
examination results, entrance into privileged professions
etc. should correspond to their ratio to the population as a
whole. (That this criterion did not apply to British West
Indian members of our Olympic squad, or to Asian 'over-
representation' in house ownership or higher education was
conveniently ignored.) Failure to meet this test was asserted
to be an indication of pervasive racism in the organisation
concerned. Any criticism of this view suggesting that there
are other relevant factors, such as lack of aptitude, or
qualifications, or even simple, personal preference is met
with the accusation of "blaming the victim" Yet this is to
evade the fundamental question of whether there is anybody
to blame in the first place. There is a confusion here of
causation with blame. It is an aspect of the scapegoatism,
which has wrought havoc with the American and,
increasingly, our legal system, namely the doctrine that any
misfortune or perceived misfortune must be due to some
unjust act by some other person or agency, who or which
must be brought to book and forced to make restitution.

Demeaning and damaging

It doesn't call for unusual powers of perception to see that
the quota regime demeans every individual ethnic achievement, which is easily attributed to legal favouritism rather
than to worth, skill or striving. Besides, such a policy cannot fail to promote huge resentments among those in the
non-ethnic majority who are better qualified, notably for
plum jobs, but who, with reason, feel unfairly victimised
by the quota rule. Quotas are often justified as a means of
helping the more unfortunate, 'disadvantaged' members of
society, but, as the black American economist, Thomas

Sowell, has shown, within the groups designated for preferential treatment the major beneficiaries are those who are already better off. This makes sense because the, usually ambitious, intellectuals who are the leading advocates of preferential policies tend to be the ones who land the big prizes like high-salaried posts. Moreover, the imposition of any standard other than merit for choosing those who perform economic tasks must decrease efficiency. And this is without considering the disruption and expense to commercial enterprises, which often capitulate to vexatious demands to avoid the hassle and expense of going to court.

As I originally went on to say, such so-called 'anti-racist' policies not only undermine freedom of contract, but, in all sorts of ways, menace personal freedom too. For example, the taboos on words often used in a totally harmless context — which in one case led to a left wing London council banning the use of road signs announcing "accident black spot" — have made certain areas of speech into a minefield as indeed are certain kinds of jokes — about Irishmen for example. The absurdity of such nannyism may make us laugh, but it has an ominous Orwellian ring. It is all the more menacing because our race laws have a special status introduced by the Race Relations Act of 1976, which swept away the principle of intention in the case of a racist offence, thus violating what has been long considered a vital principle of law — that intention should be established beyond reasonable doubt.

Censorship

Finally, without resort to law, activists have established a de facto anti-racist censorship in journalism, television, libraries and publishing through codes of conduct or taboos, all the more potent for not being spelt out but tantamount to thought control.

Developments in the Last Decade

Race lobby consolidates

The Thatcher and Major administrations did little to rein
in the race-relations establishment. The somewhat half-
hearted campaign against quangos of the early years left
the CRE unscathed. Such pussyfooting was partly because
the Tories had other priorities for reform but it also reflected their anxiety to avoid any move which would lay
them open to accusations of racism. The CRE was meanwhile quietly building up its authority by zealously back-
ing any resort to the courts by individuals claiming racial
discrimination against themselves. Any victory provided
the precedent for future claims and enabled the CRE to
extend its power into new areas. One case, the significance
of which I missed in my first foray into the subject, concerned the claim of a Sikh that his son was a victim of
racial discrimination by a private school which would not
allow the youngster to wear a turban because it was not
part of the compulsory school uniform. The High court
and Appeal Court threw out the claim on the ground that
Sikhism was a Religion not a race as defined by the Race
Relations Act of 1976, and the boy could not claim protection under that Act. Amazingly, however, in 1983 the Law
Lords thought otherwise and widened the meaning of the
word "race" far beyond its normal usage. In consequence,
as Ray Honeyford pointed out in a letter to *The
Times*(19.1.2001) "Henceforth "race" was to be used to
cover an incredible range of human groups. Virtually every
human characteristic could be prayed in aid of claiming
ethnic minority status: place of origin, history, social customs, religion, a common language, a common literature
being a member of an oppressed group. This judgement
was a godsend to the race relations lobby. It enabled the

CRE to launch a research project into the position of the Irish and to conclude , when the study was published in 1997, that the Irish were indeed a persecuted minority entitled to the CRE's protection and this has now been confirmed in case law.

Admittedly, the CRE lost some clout when the Tories abolished the Greater London Council and the Inner London Education Authority and took a firmer grip on the finances of local authorities, thus restricting support for some of the excesses of anti-racist mania. They also tightened immigration controls. Yet in John Major's last year of office, the Tories' Campaign Guide boasted about their government's increase of CRE funding to £15 million a year. They also left in place and allowed to consolidate the section 11 funding of well over £100 million a year. This provided at local level a special service for immigrants which encouraged and perpetuated separatism and discriminated against the host population in favour of racially defined groups. The opportunity to curb the race relations bureaucracy was thus lost.

With the arrival in power of Labour, wedded as it was to all forms of political correctness, the CRE had some reason to feel that its ship had come in. It adopted a more aggressive posture, increasingly pushing the view that only whites are racist. Also, through its status as the government-approved expert on race relations, it was able — through propaganda in schools and universities and by recommending and issuing codes of conduct to all and sundry — to introduce quotas by stealth under the guise of equal opportunities policies and make anti-racist courses more widely obligatory.

Aggressive and Offensive CRE

In late 1998 the CRE ran a poster campaign displaying deeply offensive racial stereotypes. The object of this exercise was apparently to fill members of the British public with disgust and self-reproach and shame them into recognising that they were rotten with racial hatred. Happily it was a flop. The CRE was itself hauled before the Advertising Standards Authority for promoting racial hatred. Interestingly enough it was revealed at around the same time, by former CRE Commissioner Ms. Blondel Cluff, a City solicitor, with the support of at least one other Commissioner, that racial hatred was rife between the Asian and Afro-Caribbean Commissioners within the CRE itself. This episode illustrates what has become the role of the CRE bureaucrats, namely to propagate the idea that Britain is desperately and increasingly racist and thereby to maximise the demand for their services as racial consultants. Yet, as Ms. Cluff went on to point out, the Commission was devoted to perpetuating its own existence rather than doing anything useful. She also questioned its active promotion of court cases, a "dangerous approach", which ignored the "harmonious relationship" between different ethnic groups and introduced instead a "litigious and aggressive attitude towards race relations". She particularly condemned its issue of a "youth card" describing how the organisation helps win "justice" in cases of discrimination. "This is ambulance-chasing, isn't it?" she said. In addition, she accused the CRE of incompetence. She cited one example which took place after she left: it authorised a preposterous series of advertisements designed to counter racism, but which were actually insulting to black people. One showed a black basketball player leaping to put the ball in the net alongside an orang-outan, leaping in the same pose towards a branch. "Born to be agile" ran the caption. "Can you imagine the kind of taunts some children would have been subjected to?" Cluff asked.

Crude propaganda

Ms. Cluff was particularly critical of the propaganda of

the CRE and its satellites claiming that British society is universally racist, whereas in fact relations between the races in Britain have improved markedly. Thus, in contrast with many of our European neighbours, in some of which, like France, avowedly racist parties manage to collect more than 15 per cent of the vote in national elections, Britain's parliament contains not a single racist party MP. Sad to relate, such considerations do not weigh with most race relations bureaucrats, who are not too scrupulous about concocting evidence to show that racism is increasing. A shocking example of such deceit appeared in a report of the findings of an employment tribunal in the case of Anthony Tang, an official responsible for coordinating Birmingham City Council's campaign against racial harassment. He was "threatened, bullied and cajoled" by his superiors in their attempts to make him fabricate figures to show that the number of racial harassment incidents in the city had soared by 150 per cent, though some of them wanted him to make the growth look even greater. This was in order to justify the authority's expenditure on anti-racism campaigns. When he refused, they insulted him, made derogatory references to his Chinese origins and finally sacked him. In the event, the tribunal decided against the council, which faced a bill of £300,000 in compensation, back pay, severance and legal costs. This was not the only example of such faking to come to light. In 1998 Hackney Council had to pay out £360,000 in a similar case (*Sunday Telegraph* 21.1.01.). But in how many other cities and boroughs up and down the land have such frauds gone undetected?

Hypocrisy

Such problems at local level, of bureaucrats who are supposed to promote good race relations deliberately seeking to aggravate them, are bad enough, but they shrink into insignificance compared to those posed by the shameless self-aggrandisement and hypocrisy of the Commission for Racial Equality.

As a taxpayer-financed quango (quasi-national government organisation) it should of course be politically neutral. Yet its party-political bias is even more pronounced. As Raj Chandran, a former commissioner wrote in the *Daily Mail* (23.4.01) "four years ago, there were three of us commissioners who had Conservative sympathies. Not an excessive number, you may have thought. I, a former parliamentary candidate was one of them. But, as our terms expired we were purged and replaced by people more sympathetic to this Government's agenda." One reason why he was sacked, he believed, was because he expressed his dissatisfaction with the autocratic way in which the organisation was being run by the then chairman Sir Herman Ouseley, who, he suggested in the *Daily Mail* should himself be sacked. He also publicly criticised the CRE for stigmatising the white majority population and stirring up resentment among Britain's black and Asian minorities. He claimed that the CRE was perpetuating two myths: first that racism, prejudice and discrimination was entirely due to whites: second that the ethnic minorities are a single group bound together by their experience of prejudice and discrimination.

CRE Labour's Poodle

However the failure to reappoint a commissioner did not depend on the chairman but on the Home Secretary Jack Straw. It is quite obvious that, since Labour took power, the CRE has been packed with Labour party poodles. Insiders have admitted that 10 of the 14 commissioners are either members of or linked to the Labour Party, sit on Government quangos or advisory committees or work as trade union activists. When pressed on the matter a Home

Office spokesman could not name a single commissioner with links to any party other than Labour. Questioned about this lack of political neutrality, the Home Office produced a reply worthy of Sir Humphrey Appleby in his heyday. This was that, since the CRE was a non-political body, there was no need to maintain political balance — though it did check with all would-be members what their politics were. It is of course conceivable that the commissioners, despite their background, would nevertheless consider it their duty to be impartial, but alas, such altruism was in short supply. As the *Daily Telegraph* revealed, the CRE refused to investigate at least 20 allegations of racism against the Labour Party.(29.4.1.)

The Pledge Plot

Given this extreme political bias, it was no surprise that, on the eve of the 2001 General Election, the CRE should, apparently in cahoots with the Labour party, seek to trap the Conservatives into appearing either to be racist or to have a weak leadership unable to control its racist element. Labour's interest in all this was to divert attention from the frightful mess it had made of immigration policy, on which it feared, as opinion polls were to confirm, it was vulnerable to Conservative attacks. Its ploy took the form of asking all the political parties to sign a pledge to reject all kinds of racial violence, racial harassment and unlawful racial discrimination and repudiate all intention to stir up racial or religious hatred. What made the whole exercise ridiculous from the word go was the fact that the behaviour they were being asked to desist from was illegal under the Race Relations Act 1976, the Public Order Act 1986 and the Human Rights Act 1998. It was also insulting. As a *Daily Telegraph* editorial said, it was like demanding that bridge players promise not to cheat at cards. The right way for MPs to treat all such pledges, which pressure groups ask them to sign, is to throw them in the wastepaper basket. Nevertheless all the party leaders signed. William Hague did so after being given an undertaking that no pressure would be put on other Tory MPs to follow suit. However it did not take long for the chairman of the CRE, Gurbux Singh, to come forward with a further demand that all Conservative candidates should endorse his pledge. Too late, Hague saw the trap into which he had fallen. He sought a compromise under which his party's candidates, while not compelled, were invited to sign. Some refused, including, it eventually transpired, the shadow chancellor Michael Portillo, which, of course, gave Labour an opportunity to deride their opponents' divisions and suggest that there was a Tory leadership crisis. In any case Gurbux Singh showed himself in his true colours in going back on his word and, without consulting the 13 other members of the commission, publishing the names of all those MPs who signed — shaming by implication all those who did not. (*Daily Mail* 23.4.01).

Robin Masala Cook

Right on cue, just as the list of names of signatories of the anti-racist pledge rolled off the CRE's website, Foreign Office aides began briefing friendly newspapers about a forthcoming speech by Foreign Secretary Robin Cook to a Left-wing think tank. In it he took the opportunity to attack the views of a an obscure but respected backbencher, John Townend, Conservative MP for Yorkshire East, who had made a speech about how immigration had changed the character of Britain, claiming that the "homogeneous Anglo-Society" had been "seriously undermined" by mass immigration. Hague promptly disowned him and pointed out that Townend's remarks were in conflict with the compact he had signed. This did not inhibit Cook, who swung into action, finding an easy target in Townend's views of

Britain as a homogeneous society, pointing out that Britain had, over the centuries taken in many immigrants and that Townend had pitifully misread our history. Too bad that Cook himself went over the top suggesting that the British had never been a race, (which is quite arguable if the criterion is purely biological) but implying further, in tune with the Brussels-style federalism I have referred to earlier, that we had no real national identity at all. His pronouncement that membership of the EU strengthened rather than weakened British identity was mere juggling with words when what he was campaigning for was our absorption and effective disappearance as a nation in a European superstate. (In any case, if race is a myth, what business did his Government have distributing at the time of his speech census forms with more racial and ethnic categories than ever before? These provided boxes for the Irish, Welsh and Scottish and Caribbeans to declare their distinctness, but left none for the English majority!) He went on to brand the Tories racists and by contrast enthused about Britain's multicultural society of which he claimed, rather trivially, Britain's most popular dish was 'chicken tikka masala' was the symbol. This spurred Townend to make a further series of remarks complaining about our becoming a mongrel race. This incited the only black Tory member of the House of Lords, Lord Taylor, into berating Hague for weak leadership because he did not immediately withdraw the whip from Townend. Actually Hague thought that to do so was pointless as, in any case, Townend was retiring at the election. It was not clear whether or not Lord Taylor was conspiring with Labour and preparing to make a dramatic crossing of the floor of the House. In the end, however, Hague managed to effect a compromise by which Townend apologised and Taylor affirmed his loyalty to the party.

CRE Discredited

This episode reflected badly on the CRE. It was an all too typical example of the kind of self-righteous, self-important intervention in politics in which it is inclined to indulge, inflaming rather than defusing racial tensions. In this case, its meddling was compounded by what had every appearance of being shameful collusion with the Labour party. Labour was happy to cooperate because it was trying to cover up its loss of control of illegal immigration and saw the pledge as a means of diverting public attention by directing accusations of racism at its Conservative opponents. It was also one more notch in the trend towards the suppression of free speech. After all, as A.N.Wilson pointed out, (*Sunday Telegraph* 6.5.01) "Mr Townend was saying what most people's grandparents say". We have come a long way from Voltaire's pronouncement "I detest what he says, but I will lay down my life to defend his right to say it".

Yet justice does sometimes prevail. In the end the CRE/Labour plot backfired. Ex-chairman of the CRE, Sir Herman Ouseley, sharply criticised Labour's record on race and pointedly avoided criticising Conservative MPs who refused to sign the pledge. There were leaks, apparently from the office of Gordon Brown, supremo of Labour's election campaign and also an old enemy of Cook, to the effect that the Foreign Secretary's speech had been a blunder. In fact it was worse: a cynical attempt to stir up the race issue for party advantage and in direct conflict with the pledge which Labour had just signed. The Labour hierarchy seems to think it owns the ethnic vote and has a right to exploit racist incidents to consolidate it. Among such incidents a tragic and harrowing one, which happened nine years earlier, stands out and its ramifications are still with us today.

The Lawrence murder

For racial minorities, Britain is one of the safest places in the world to live. Tragically however racist crimes do occur, the best known of recent times being the murder of the teenager, Stephen Lawrence, on 22 April 1993 when the Major government was in its last throes. He was set upon by a gang of white youths crying 'What. What! Nigger!' and stabbed, fatally, by the leading thug. The culprits were never brought to book. His parents, who were role models of self-improving working people, were devastated, understandably bitter and determined not to let the police get away with a cover-up of their incompetence and consequent failure to find and prosecute the murderers. Their grief aroused widespread sympathy and justified anger.

Less deserving of sympathy were the representatives of various antiracist lobby groups, including the Anti-Racist Alliance, the Anti-Nazi League and the Black Panthers, who descended on the Lawrences from the word go, seeing the tragedy as a long-awaited chance, if they could manipulate the murdered boy's family, to push their agenda. A complaint by Neville and Doreen Lawrence to the Police Complaints Authority about the inadequacy of the police handling of the crime led to a thorough examination of what had happened by a score or so of officers of Kent Constabulary. They found that the performance by the Metropolitan Police had not been up to an acceptable standard but could trace no evidence that police racism had interfered with their investigation. The *Daily Mail* ran a campaign for the Lawrence family to obtain justice and the parents of Stephen Lawrence, in an attempt to remedy the failure of the police to prosecute the murderers, brought their own private prosecution, on 17 April 1996, but this failed. In a statement at the subsequent inquest the distraught Doreen Lawrence claimed that the suspects at the private trial had been acquitted because the Crown Court had been staged. The purpose of the rigged acquittal was to make a clear statement to the black community that their lives were worth nothing. The system of British justice, she said, supported any white person who wished to commit murder against any black person. Her son had been stereotyped by the police as a criminal and a gang member because he was black. 'Our crime was living in a country where the justice system supports racist murders against innocent people'. (Preface by Norman Dennis to Racist Murder and Pressure-Group Politics, Civitas, September 2000). They then sued 42 serving and former Metropolitan Police Officers, including the off-duty constable who tried to help Stephen after the stabbing. This the Daily Mail regretfully felt bound to condemn in a leader, headlined "Must this Crusade Become a Vendetta?"

Macpherson rampant

In June 1997, shortly after Labour's victory in the General Election, the Macpherson inquiry was announced by the new Home Secretary Jack Straw. Its task was to inquire into matters arising from the death of Stephen Lawrence and to establish what lessons could be learned from the investigation and prosecution of racially-motivated crimes. These terms of reference, implied that the murder of Stephen Lawrence was, above all else, a racially-motivated crime and not, for instance, as was plausibly believed by some police officers involved in the initial inquiry, a product of free-floating aggression by thugs who would as willingly have chosen a white victim. They amounted to an invitation to treat racist crimes as of special significance in our society requiring a delving into its causes and treatment by the authorities with a view to shaping government policy in the future. As we shall see, the response to the invitation would not disappoint those who had issued it.

As Lord Skidelsky commented after studying the eventual report, the conclusion to which he was irresistibly led was "that the judge and his advisers knew from the start that this was how they were going to interpret the botched police investigation, in the wider interest, as they conceived it, of better race relations." (*The Review, The Journal of the Social Market Foundation*, August 1999). Sir William Macpherson, the chairman, became more and more insistent as the inquiry proceeded that the murder was a "purely" racist one. Indeed, he condemned any suggestion, notably by police officers, that there were any motives for the murder other than racism, as itself proof of racist thinking, and of "institutional racism" in those who dared to put it forward. This was not an argument but a form of intimidation, strongly reminiscent of the bullying technique used by Stalin's judge, Andrei Vyshinsky, during the show trials of leading Bolsheviks.

The Court

The public inquiry had the appearance of a judicial proceeding, but failed to uphold some crucial practices normal in English law. Rules of evidence were modified. The tone was not so much that of an inquiry, more an indictment of the police, though of course they were not on trial for anything. There were over a score of barristers, many of them QCs, Witnesses were examined, cross-examined and harassed not only by counsel but by the barracking crowd of anti-police groups in the public gallery, who often behaved like the mob in the trials in Jacobin clubs during the French revolution. An old-style Marxist would have enjoyed the spectacle of the fat cats of the legal profession brandishing their forensic skills at the expense of the humble constables and sergeants and gleefully filed it for future reference as a prize example of upper-class nastiness towards the proles. Particularly odious was the pressure put on police witnesses to confess to their own racist thoughts and beliefs, testify to the racist thoughts of other people and admit that they and their colleagues were collectively guilty of 'institutional' or unwitting racism. Yet exposing such thought crime has never been part of the English judicial process. It evoked eerie memories of show trials in Nazi Germany and Stalin's Russia in which it was not enough to find the accused guilty: they had to be humiliated as well.

Macpherson's 'Experts'

In Part II of the inquiry, the Macpherson "evidence" came from written and oral representatives of advocates, authors and advocacy groups. This too was a glorious opportunity for anti-police intellectuals and pressure groups.

One expert to whom Macpherson deferred was the black revolutionary Stokeley Carmichael, the inventor of the phrase "institutional racism", (which, as we shall see, was to provide the cornerstone of Macpherson's conclusions in his final report). According to Carmichael the phrase "originates in the operation of established and respected forces in society". It was strange that, in his anti-racist musings, Macpherson should defer to this man who was not only an opponent of Martin Luther King, but deeply and overtly racist. He was especially anti-semitic. One of his favourite sayings was "The only good Zionist is a dead Zionist". He called for all out war with Israel and declared: "We must take a lesson from Hitler."

Another 'expert' to win Macpherson's warm approval was Dr Robin Oakley whose concept of 'institutional' was far removed from normal usage. Examples of institutional racism in the conventional sense would be in South Africa under Apartheid or fifty years ago in the American southern states where laws, customs and routine police behaviour were designed to favour the whites. For Oakley,

however, 'institutional racism' was not overt but unconscious. It was covert, subtle, hidden, invisible and undetected, indeed undetectable by ordinary means. As the
Civitas authors remarked in their study: "Who can see what
is invisible? Only the adepts of the anti-racist illuminati."
(*Racist Murder and Pressure Group Politics*, by Norman
Dennis, George Eidos and Ahmed Al-Shahi, Civitas, Institute for the Study of Civil Society 2000). On the basis of
this will-o-the-wisp category of racism, the existence of
which could not be proved or disproved by evidence,
Oakley pronounced that institutional racism was found in
the police though in no way confined to them but was 'pervasive throughout the culture and institutions of the whole
of British society.'

It was also extraordinary that Macpherson showed no
embarrassment at taking evidence from the Metropolitan
Police Service Black Police Association — a black-only
body, which, by definition should be described, if anything
can, as a racist institution. Any white organisation which
refused entry to blacks would have the book thrown at it.
The only way of defending this inconsistency is on the
outrageous assumption that only whites are racist.

The Macpherson Report

In February 1999 The report of the Macpherson inquiry
into the Metropolitan police handling of the Lawrence
murder investigation was published. It pronounced that
there had been fundamental errors in the investigation of
the murder and that these were caused by chronic
organisational failure, institutional, or unwitting, racism
and failures of leadership. It concluded that institutional
racism existed in other police forces and indeed other
institutions countrywide. Yet the report produced not s shred
of evidence of racism on the part of the police. Nor did it
even attempt to show that the structure of the Metropolitan

Police Service was such as to put ethnic minorities at a disadvantage. Nor did it produce evidence that individual officers dealing with the murder of Stephen Lawrence had displayed racism, other than what Macpherson called the 'offensive' use of the word 'coloured' which is no longer fashionable in professional anti-racist circles (conveniently ignoring the fact that one of the main black civil rights organisations in the United States is called The National Assocaition for the Advancement of Colored Peoples'). No evidence was produced to show that the police would have handled the case differently had the victim been white. The conclusion was not based on evidence but on the inference, which Macpherson chose to make, on the basis of all that he had heard and read in the course of the inquiry. Yet, as we have seen, this inference was not founded on facts produced in court but seems to have been derived from the opinions of so-called 'experts' who did not produce any facts either. The other basis of Macpherson's inference of pervasive racism in the police and throughout British society seems to be first: his own eccentric definition of racism (in chapter 6 of his report) as anything which is perceived to be racist either by the victim or a third party. This idea that the perception of a fact makes it a fact was well described by Lord Skidelsky as 'a legal and philosophical monstrosity.' (*The Review. Journal of the the Social Market Foundation*, August 1999) It is indeed, for, if made the basis of legislation, it would mean that the mere accusation of racism by anyone would automatically be tantamount to evidence of guilt, with the accuser being judge and jury. The kindest interpretation of how Macpherson came to nail himself to this absurdity is that he was almost neurotically anxious to avoid giving offence to the ethnic minorities. So he arrived at the weird position that any behaviour to which they were sensitive must be racist. Of course in their behaviour, the police, with whom the report is primarily concerned, should certainly be sensitive to the feelings of the people with whom they are dealing, but that rule should not only apply to ethnics, but to everybody. Or is it OK to be rude to the non-ethnic majority?

The second basis of Macpherson's inference of rampant racism among the police and the British in general he appears to have picked up from the submission of the CRE: that racism exists wherever and whenever social institutions co-exist with racial inequalities. This is to make the silly assumption that the only cause of inequalities is race. The CRE would however like to have us believe this because that would be the open sesame for imposing racial quotas for everything under the sun.

Macpherson's Recommendations

The report went on to make 70 recommendations. Among the more disturbing were the following:

- Review and revision of race awareness training to apply to all PCs including CID and civilian staff.

- Records to be made of all stops and searches, showing reason for stop, outcome, self-defined ethnic identity of the person concerned. A record to be given to the person stopped.

- The Home Secretary and police authorities to adopt targets for recruitment, progression and retention of minority ethnic staff, these to be reported regularly and published. Targets are of course another name for quotas.

- Racist language or behaviour and possession of offensive weapons in a private place to be made a criminal offence.

- Chief Officers of Police to be vicariously liable for the

acts and omissions of their officers.

- Racial incidents to be defined by the victims rather than police officers. *They are racist if the victim says that they are racist* (my italics), this definition of racist incident to be adopted by local government and "other relevant agencies".

- The "double jeopardy" rule which prevents a suspect being prosecuted for the same crime twice to be ended.

These prescriptions, including brainwashing, thought control, the definition of a crime (racism) so wide and vague that nobody would be safe from false accusation and conviction and the abolition of one of the oldest safeguards of the liberty of the subject, are what we might expect to find in a totalitarian regime. As Lord Skidelsky put it 'So fanatic is the report's determination to stamp out 'unwitting racism' that it is willing to contemplate the imposition of a police state to achieve its aims'. Such fanaticism has not been something one has been accustomed to find in a British judge — at least not since Judge Jeffreys.

The overall thrust of the report is decidedly Orwellian. The idea for instance that people using racist language in a private place should be prosecuted could spell the end of privacy and the bugging of private premises as a matter of routine. This sort of prying would logically lead to children being encouraged to report any racist remarks at home to their teachers as part of their "race awareness" training. It would also provide ample opportunities for the blackmailer. Then again, the definition of a racist incident as "any incident which is perceived to be racist by the victim or any other person" is not only ridiculous but sinister. As Frank Ellis eloquently and pertinently puts it (*The Macpherson Report, 'Anti-racist' hysteria and the Sovietisation of the United Kingdom*, Right Now Press 2001): "This is a charter for every malicious and vindictive type to make trouble, the sort , who in the former Soviet Union and STASI-infected East Germany, would denounce their neighbours for making critical remarks about Stalin or Honecker, in the hope of securing some material advantage or avenge some real or imagined slight. We should ask ourselves whether we want to live in a society where every utterance has to be weighed before we speak, where all verbal spontaneity is lost, where we speak in soundbites and officially-approved slogans. Such a society would, in effect, fall silent, its citizens fearful that anything they say could be used against them by the Thought Police and self-appointed seekers after "hate crimes". The Macpherson definition of racism is more than just an attack on free speech: it is an attack on speech itself, that most wonderful of man's faculties. Is this what we want?"

As Dr Frank Ellis also points out, the vicarious liability of Senior Police Officers for failures of subordinates with regard to racist incidents is recommended to apply also to "other relevant agencies". This could have devastating effects on freedom of expression by academics. Liability might extend to left wing dons for making disparaging remarks about Americans. It is to be expected that, under such a regime, university administrations, already cravenly weak-kneed on any issues connected with race or multiculturalism and fearful of being vicariously liable for ideas expressed by members of the faculty, will rush to adopt a policy of vetting before allowing publication of written work or lectures by staff members. This could be made to apply to the internet as well.

The Witch-hunt Mentality

Yet, as Hugh Trevor-Roper has pointed out, when a collective psychosis grips a society, even some of its most distinguished members may become its keenest proponents. Thus, during the witch craze of the 16th and 17th centuries

— the age, remember, of the renaissance and the Newtonian scientific revolution when the modern enlightenment is supposed to have begun — hundreds of thousands, perhaps millions of mostly deluded old women were burnt to death for allegedly casting spells causing thunderstorms or hail or stealing milk or butter during what were said to be their frequent night rides on broomsticks. Did the great thinkers of the time condemn this superstition and cruelty? On the contrary "some of the most original and cultivated intellectuals" not only accepted the theory of witchcraft and its abominations, " but positively devoted their genius to its propagation" Thus France's Jean Bodin, the Aristotle of the 16th century, wrote a book about sorcery in 1580, which more than any other stoked up the witch fires throughout Europe. It demanded death not only for witches but for all who did not believe in every detail of the new demonology (including attendance at the witches' Sabbath, spitting on the cross, and engaging in orgies of drink and sex with demons or with the devil himself, who appeared sometimes as a huge bearded man clothed in black, at others as a goat or a huge toad.). Of course there was no proof of guilt on any of these amazing charges, the ordinary rules of evidence being suspended, as were the ordinary limits on torture, which was ferociously applied until they confessed. (*The European Witch-Craze of the 16th and 17th Centuries* by H.R.Trevor-Roper, Penguin Peregrine 1978)

Macpherson Report's Pernicious Effects

The report was initially welcomed by all the political parties, more, it seemed as a reflex than as a considered response, especially by the Tories. The unintended effects, however, were not long in appearing. In December 2000 an independent report by former Home Office researcher, Dr. Marion Fitzgerald, showed that, following the Macpherson Report, stopping and searching by the Met had fallen by nearly a half and street crime had soared. This was seized upon by Tory leader William Hague in a strong speech blaming the Macpherson Report for damaging the morale of the police and preventing them from doing their job of keeping law and order. As he pointed out, the British Crime Survey for the year 2000 (*Daily Telegraph* 15.12.00) indicated robberies up 14%, muggings up 4% and violence against a stranger up 29%. He was immediately and predictably branded a racist, by Stephen Lawrence's father, Prime Minister Tony Blair and Home Secretary Jack Straw, though a careful reading of his speech showed that it was not in the least racist. His main argument was perfectly reasonable: that use of powers of stop and search had proved a useful means of reducing crime and a restriction of those powers led to an increase in crime.

Stop and search fiasco

However, after the vilification of the whole Metropolitan police force by Macpherson, policemen on the beat had to watch their step. Apart from the danger of being accused of racism in any incident involving a member of an ethnic minority, the extra form-filling and reporting required according to the Macpherson recommendations which the Home secretary had accepted in full, made the stopping and searching one of them more troublesome as well as more risky. So why bother? Moreover the contention that police searches were biased, which had been a staple criticism of the force since the Scarman report and had been accepted uncritically by Macpherson, were shown by a study, based on research in London and several other English cities, to be mistaken. When compared to the available as opposed to the resident population there was no indication of bias against ethnic minorities. On the contrary, white people tended to be stopped and searched in higher numbers than their numbers in the available population would suggest. Sir William Macpherson denied that his report led to an increase in street robberies, said that all his report had done was to argue that there should not be discrimination in stop and search but pointed out that six times as many black men as white men were stopped. However it was naïve of him not to see that his report 's suggestion that existing stop and search policy was racist (as the subsequent evidence above shows that it was not) was bound to inhibit its use. Also his strong emphasis on the need for the police to show more sensitivity towards the feelings of blacks than whites as good as told the police to mind their back. (*Daily Telegraph* 15.12.2000)

Biased Statistics, Plunging Morale

The Macpherson report had one unexpected result — a massive rise in racist incidents recorded by the police. Did this mean that its pronouncements had stimulated hatred of ethnic minorities and made British society more racist? Not really, but there was a very real sense in which it affected the statistics of racism. This was due to the report's absurd definition of a racist incident as one that was perceived to be racist by the victim or any third person. For the police have ever since been obliged to abide by this bit of tomfoolery so that any altercation between people, which any passer-by perceives to be racist is recorded as such. Thus officers are logging crimes as racist that have as much or more to do with gang fights, boredom, alcohol and drugs. Result: — a rise of 107 per cent in racist incidents in the year 2001. (Charlotte Metcalf , *Daily Telegraph* 16.5.01). Why, one may ask, are the police recording crimes as racist which have nothing to do with racism except on Macpherson;s daft definition? Surely because they have been so demoralised by the report's blanket accusation of racism being institutionalised in the whole British police force that the men in blue dare not raise objections to this idiocy but find it safer and easier to go along with it. Needless to say, post-Macpherson the morale of the police sank and recruitment suffered too. Who wants to join a police force which has been held up to public scorn as a racist institution? It was significant that the Metropolitan Police who were the main target for the strictures of Macpherson saw a decline of 5 per cent in their strength in the six months to the end of September 2000 — a drop of 1,241 to 12,444 at a time when numbers in the rest of the country stood still. The politically correct however had something to be pleased about — the recruitment of ethnic minority officers rose significantly especially in the Met, which was responsible for half of the 11 per cent increase of ethnics recruited nationally. Efficiency also declined, with police officers concerned more with demonstrating their political correctness over racism than with roping in lawbreakers. Most ominous perhaps was the evidence of Left-wing thinking in the Met, especially among the brighter, more ambitious upper ranks who could see which way the wind is blowing. They could hardly be expected to take a stand against the official doctrine so dear to their political masters. Thus, when in March 2001 William Hague expressed concern about the Macpherson report, pointing out that it had had the effect of reducing stop and search with a resulting surge in street crime, he was denounced, along with "the right wing lobby", in the *Guardian* by Superintendent Ali Dizaei. A *Daily Telegraph* editorial listed several other examples of this Leftism in the police force, perhaps the most sinister being a pronouncement by Paul Wilson of the Black Police Association.

Wilson was quoted as speaking of the need for whites to be "coerced" or "compelled" to give up power. The editorial warned, as well it might, of the "real danger — that the victims of particular kinds of crime are going to be given preferential treatment. And it will be determined according to which lobby group shouts loudest. Unless someone speaks up for the great silent majority, Bonfire of the Vanities-style law enforcement will be the wave of the future." (*Daily Telegraph* 27.3.01)

This comment incidentally raises a further question:- What justification can there be for having a Black Police Association? Admittedly its charter states that "the term black does not denote skin colour but is used as a political term to emphasise the common experience of individuals opposing the effects of racism" — but this is as remote from normal usage as Macpherson's definition of racist behaviour — as what the victim or any third person perceives it to be. Is it conceivable that a White Police Association, could be set up, whatever its charter might say, without its members being hounded out of the force?

Loss of Public Esteem

It can be no coincidence that Macpherson's vilification of the police as institutionally racist and the pressure put on them to give higher priority to political correctness than to catching crooks has led to a serious decline in public confidence in them. According to research by Professor Mike Hough, Director of the criminal policy research unit at the South Bank University only 20 per cent of the public believed that the police were doing a good job compared with 40 per cent in 1982. His explanation was that people felt that the police spent too little of their time on dealing with the things which concern them personally like crime and burglary. This halving of confidence in the police apparently has gone hand in hand with a growth in fear of becoming a victim of crime. This the Professor interpreted as being partly due to the fact that violent crime was rising, even though recorded crime as a whole was falling. However he also thought that it was due to plunging police morale, reflected during the 2001 general election when rank and file police officers heckled Home Secretary Jack Straw. (*Daily Express* 22.5.2001)

CPS Infected

It is not only the police who have been distracted by this obsession with racism from their central duty of upholding and enforcing the law: it has also apparently smitten the Crown Prosecution Service, if we are to judge by its role in a recent case, arising from a playground fracas at an Ipswich primary school. This involved a plump white 10-year-old boy thumping an Asian classmate for calling him a "Teletubby". It beggars belief that, following a complaint to the police by the Asian boy's parents, the Crown Prosecution Service actually went to the lengths of charging the white youngster with racially-aggravated assault. The CPS resisted a High Court attempt to block the prosecution — the judge commented that the CPS was using a sledgehammer to crack a nut — and only dropped the charge "in the public interest" after the boy's lawyers indicated that he would plead guilty to common assault. The boy was given an absolute discharge by Ipswich Youth Court. However the cost of bringing the case was £20,000 of public money, the CPS's request for the white boy's parents to pay £50 towards costs being rejected. The question irresistibly springs to mind:- Whatever happened to commonsense? (*Daily Telegraph* 12.5.01.)

Humbug

The humbug, which pervaded the official response to the Lawrence murder was startlingly illustrated in November 2000 when a 10-year-old Nigerian boy, Damilola Taylor, was stabbed to death in Peckham. The case was in many respects parallel with that of young Stephen Lawrence. Both boys were bright young blacks with good prospects who were callously killed by street gangs in an urban ghetto.

Yet, while there was a great hue and cry from the professional anti-racists over the former, leading as we have seen to a cutback on stop and search and the branding of the whole Metropolitan police force as institutionally racist, the latter, apart from a few pious pronouncements, was practically ignored. Why? — Because Stephen Lawrence was killed by whites, whereas Damilola Taylor was killed by blacks. The assumption was — despite evidence that ethnic tensions between Africans and West Indians may have played a part in Damilola's victimisation — that racism played no part in the murder. This is just another example of what might be called the slogan of the anti-racist lobby: that only white people are racists.

Illogical

This illustrates the logical absurdities with which the whole doctrine of racial justice is riddled. It is invariably asymmetrical. It is only applied against European behaviour towards non-Europeans (or Christians towards heathens, or English towards Celtic fringes) never the hostility directed towards the English/Christian/European core. It is not about individual representatives of minority groups behaving badly towards each other; it's the new lament about inequality that has replaced the moaning about social class earlier in the 20th century. It is OK for the lower classes to hate and express hatred for the upper crust but not vice versa — hatred is the privilege of failure.

Again anti-racism nearly always lumps together all manner of diverse peoples in a single amorphous group, called "the ethnic minority", as when the police are supposed to recruit 25% ethnic minorities in London to match the composition of the population. What can it mean? If 25% of the population were Jamaican, how would that please the Hindus or Chinese? Why do they not specify quotas for each group separately? From the point of view of a Chinese, or indeed a Nigerian, a Jamaican is probably more alien than a Scot. Minorities have little in common, except as seen by racist anti-racists, who define them as non-white: defined, that is to say, purely in relation to the majority. (Since I originally wrote this I've been told that in some London boroughs the left wing councils do have quotas for every ethnic group — the great advantage of this from the anti-racist lobby's point of view is that it increases the demand and therefore the number of jobs for race relations bureaucrats).

Vaz's vindicators

Thus, in February, 2001, when Europe Minister, Keith Vaz, was being investigated by the press over alleged corruption, a letter appeared in the Mirror and the Guardian from Lord Platel of Blackburn, Lord King of West Bromwich and other leading Asian and black eminences writing "As members of the Asian and black community..." claimed to feel "a deep sense of unease and hurt over the fact that Britain's first elected Asian minister is being subjected to a campaign of denigration and fear on the long-term impact on the " good community relations we have fought so hard to achieve." As *Daily Telegraph* sketch-writer, Frank Johnson impishly remarked, "Some of us had not realised that only one community was what Asians and blacks comprised. We thought it was two. Our observation suggested that, however good their relations in general, Asians and blacks do not always get on well together." Why didn't the letter include signatories from the Chinese community, he asked, since they are equally unwhite?

Quota mania

An obsession with quotas now pervades every aspect of race relations. It was of course bound to arise in connection with the composition of the new House of Lords. It is suggested that 15% of the members should be from ethnic minorities: this probably means non-white though they are only about 6% of the population. But how is this 15% broken down between Indian, Chinese, Pakistani, African and Bangladeshi? Will it be by population, for example should it be double or more of their proportion of the population, or will some groups be favoured over others? What if a group already has members in the House of Lords? The whole quota idea is absurd.

Quotas are racist

In education there is a fuss over "under-representation" of minorities in the better bits of the system with the implication that the majority has rigged it against them. Yet here the anti-racists choose to disaggregate the figures to work a different scam. That is to say they will only mention the under-achievers (e.g. Jamaicans and Bangladeshis) and not the high-achievers (East Asians, Hindus and Sikhs) or the average (Pakistanis and Africans). As soon as you do this it is clear that racism is not a key variable — rather that cultural tradition, flexibility and family stability are the key ones. Why should we penalise Jews or Chinese or Hindus and underwrite Jamaicans and Bangladeshis? That is the logic of what the anti-racists want — not equality of opportunity but of outcome through quotas. Yet the logic of quotas is that used by anti-Semites in the past in the USA or Austria, or against the Chinese in Malaysia. Quotas are racist however they are deployed. Likewise equality is theft.

Culture plunder

Just after St. George's day, 2001, the British adopted census rules to show which ethnic group people belonged to, but, though it allowed them to say they were Scottish, while even the Welsh were encouraged to write in the word

"Welsh", it made no provision for the overwhelming 40 million majority to say they were "English". There was in fact a dazzling selection of descriptions available for everyone else, including "White", "Mixed", "Asian or Asian British", "Black or Black British" or "Chinese or other ethnic group." But what, exactly, was the point of this question about everybody's ethnicity? In the document accompanying the questionnaire, the defence given was that it would "help to uncover racial inequality and take action to tackle it". What that really meant was that it would help to establish a basis for demands for racial quotas, which, as I have shown above, is a form of pressure-group politics, which is morally indefensible and erodes the principle of equality under the law. This is another import from the US where the government spends around £130 billion a year on special provisions for minorities. However, at America's millennium census this baseline for affirmative action began to unravel. A campaign by a group of interracial families had asked that children of mixed parentage should not be required to choose between their parents and instead should be allowed to call themselves "multiracial" in a separate box on the census form. This proposal galvanised frenzied opposition from the civil rights establishment, which foresaw a gradual disappearance of the classifications which justified their existence, as the exploding increase of mixed marriages led to more and more citizens choosing the mixed race box. In the event, the mixed race box was not accepted, but the crucial decision was made that respondents could fill in more than one racial box. For official purposes it was decided that those who checked in a both white and a minority category would be counted as members of that minority. As a result the Census bureau's percentages tallied well over a hundred. It became impossible to compare the 2000 census with the 1990 count or any that came before it. For instance the numbers who counted themselves as having Indian blood went up by 65 per cent. To add to the woes of the civil rights brigade, in a *USA Today/ CNN/ Gallup* poll conducted in March 2001, 64 per cent of the public — and 75 per cent of those under 18, thought that it was "good for the country" for people to think of themselves as multiracial rather than belonging to a single race. Add to this the fact that more than 60 per cent of   all American teenagers have dated someone of another colour or ethnic group and it is clear that the perceived ethnic divisions and the conduct based on these perceptions are crumbling. As a result it is increasingly difficult to see what evidence there is to justify affirmative action.

Our hope must be that the same earthy realities of inter-marriage between races and a similar erosion of the importance popularly attached to ethnic differences, will also demolish the case for affirmative action in Britain.

Racism by institution

The most damaging legacy of the Macpherson report was the central contention that the Metropolitan Police force (and by implication British society) is institutionally racist. It shows how warped our mindset has become that an experienced judge, apparently in full possession of his faculties and not acting under obvious duress, should make a pronouncement contrary to a fundamental principle of English law — that there cannot be guilt without intent. The idea that people are fated to behave in a certain way, not out of choice but because they belong to a certain social grouping, belongs to the same family of ideas as the Marxist notion that individuals' attitudes are expressions of class interest. There is another parallel with the Freudian doctrine that our outlook is the result of unconscious sexual urges. According to such notions of social determinism, Truth, honesty, justice etc. also become relative. The principle common to these cases is that views have no intrinsic validity but are to be understood purely in terms of their origins. Unfortunately, as Karl Popper has pointed out, this ad hominem approach undermines all rational discourse. For it can be condemned and indeed dismissed on its own terms. Indeed at this juncture rational argument ceases and the issue can only be resolved by blows. The Marxist analysis can be refuted in terms of Marxist dialectic as no more than an expression of the resentments of a frustrated, unsuccessful (at least in his lifetime) lower-middle class journalist/conspirator. Freud's views may be dismissed as merely the rationalisation of his own sexual repressions (apparently he never allowed himself to be psycho-analysed). Institutional racism may plausibly be described as an idea spawned by power-hungry bureaucrats in the race relations industry and institutionalised in as well as financially focused in the CRE.

No Place in a Free Society

In any event, the idea of institutional racism has no place in a free society, as it is incompatible with individual resoinsibility and choice As *Times* columnist, Michael Gove, put it succinctly and pertinently: "For true liberals, justice means due process, not a pre-determined result and equality of access not outcome. But for the Left, as the Jewish-American David Horowitz argues, advancing equality has become a weapon to extend state power. "Just as Marxists are convinced that there is class oppression when everyone is not economically equal, so race radicals claim that oppression exists when any disparity appears between racial groups, as long that is as the disparity works against the 'oppressed'. No one argues that the diminishing presence of whites in major athletics is the result of conspiracy or requires a government subsidy." (*Times* 11.4.00.)

Britain is not a racist society. To illustrate that contention consider three historical examples of societies, which were, by common consent, racist, namely the southern states of the USA before emancipation, Nazi Germany in the 1930s and apartheid South Africa. Britain is not in the least like them, As Ray Honeyford summed up the position: "We do not underpin our institution with any odious racial theory; we do not relate civil liberties to skin colour and we do not regulate access to the welfare state according to ethnic origin. On the contrary, as far as the state is concerned, Britain positively favours its minorities in terms both of protective legislation and exclusive public funding."(*Race and Free Speech* by Ray Honeyford, Claridge Press, Blasts No. 6, 1992).

The real threat to the freedom of our society today comes not from institutional racism, which is a fantasy, but from institutional anti-racism which is verifiable and real and oppressive. No better example can be found than in social work, one of the fortresses of anti-racist thinking. To support this accusation we need look no further than the guidelines on the content and the implementation of the new Diploma in Social Work by the Central Council for Education and Training. It starts with the declaration "racism is endemic in the values, attitudes and structures of British society". Apparently colleges, which dissent from this view, will lose their licence to train social workers. In the CCET's rules the guidelines say that those in charge must ensure that all aspects of the curriculum are permeated by an anti-racist analysis. They state baldly that freedom of speech does not include freedom to express any opinions which are 'racist' or favourable to 'racism'. (*Racist Murder and pressure Group Politics*, by Norman Dennis, George Erdos and Ahmed Al-Shah, Civitas September 2000.)

Macpherson on Colour

Early on in the Macpherson report the Lawrence parents

are fulsomely praised for their statements deploring col-our-consciousness and for declaring their belief in equal-ity under the law. Later, the report does a somersault and colour blindness — treating everybody the same, becomes the problem. Police should be colour-conscious provided that this favours black people. The police should be col-our-conscious in order to take account of black sensitivity and because of their different culture. Of course the police should display sensitivity towards the members of the public with whom they deal but this sensitivity should be shown equally towards everybody, not not skewed in favour of ethnic groups. In any case Macpherson offers no evidence that there is such a thing as a cultural divide. In fact, in a recent study Tizard and Phoenix showed that no such phe-nomenon as a unitary black culture exists. (*Tizard, B. and Phoenix, A. White or Mixed Race? Race and Parentage in the Lives of Young People of Mixed Parentage.* London, Routledge 1993.) The attempt of Macpherson to give re-spectability to a sort of pro-black apartheid policy in po-lice dealings with the public is not only outrageous but absurd. The logic of his approach is that those blacks who display anti-police attitudes (because this is part of their culture) should be better-treated than those who are friendly and cooperative. A case in point was the black youngster Duwayne Brooks, who was with Stephen Lawrence at the time of his murder and swore at the police women officers when they arrived at the scene of the crime, calling them "fucking cunts" and "pigs". He was wearing a cap bearing the slogan 'Stay black' and trousers with machine-gun bullet holes sewn into them. Not surprisingly one of them, PC Joanne Smith, described his behaviour as aggressive. Yet Macpherson drew the strange conclusion that this was an example of the police racially stereo-typing him and blamed them for not showing him more sympathy.

Once accept this thoroughly racist idea that coloured

people are not equal under the law but must be treated with more sympathy than non-coloured people and this sets a precedent for a range of policies prejudicial to the majority, giving a weapon to every pressure group acting for every minority.

The Quota Mentality

The Macpherson report has undoubtedly led to an acceleration of government attempts to interfere with economic activity to bias it in favour of ethnic minorities. Increasingly the imposition of quotas as a solution to all problems of alleged racial inequalities is accepted as holy writ. Particular attention has been paid to the police. Just before the publication of the report on the Stephen Lawrence inquiry, Home Secretary Jack Straw, angry that many chief constables had failed to act on warnings issued a year before to improve race relations in their forces (Dyfed Powys was put in the dunce's corner for having only one officer from an ethnic background), ordered them to treble black and Asian recruitment and set a national target of 7 per cent of officers from ethnic minorities.(*Times* 10.2.99.) Sporadic claims of institutional racism in various national bodies have, of course, been surfacing for years, but the approach and aftermath of the Macpherson report gave them focus as well as an adrenalin boost.

Producer Capture

The Macpherson report strengthened a tendency to distort police activities to the neglect of their proper function. The permanent duty of our police forces is to serve the public, but as a result of the report's recommendations a huge proportion of their time is, in effect, given over to serving the CRE. Is this what the British people want? Surely not. The present situation of Britain's police illustrates an ever-present danger in all public services where the people have to accept what a monopoly supplier — the government — provides. This is what economists call "producer capture". If the suppliers of a service are not obliged to please the consumer (the taxpayers who fund them) power drifts into the hands of the producers, government ministers, bureaucrats, quangos unaccountable to the public and public sector unions. To test the validity of the theory in the case of the police service the Adam Smith Institute commissioned the MORI organisation to conduct a poll into how far the police actually do what the public would like them to do, as opposed to what they find it convenient to do. What it found was that the police concentrated on a 'social' agenda, which the public do not think very important.

Overwhelmingly the public wish the police to give priority to four tasks. They want action against criminal gangs and organised crime. They favour targeting muggings and street crime. They desire action to prevent burglary and to recover stolen property. They yearn for a visible police presence on the street to prevent crime. The police jump on those who defend their own property with force, but the public regards this as their least essential activity, among those listed. By another huge margin the public think the police spend far too much time and effort on enforcing motoring laws and have little use for the tougher laws on speeding and drinking which the police are for ever advocating, and would rather they gave as much time to dealing with serious crime. The strong police concern with building good relations with ethnic minority communities is among the activities which the public thinks least important. It wants the police to get on with tackling crime. Of course the public is right. In the millennial year some 190,000 more criminal offences were committed than in 1999. Violent crime rose by 16 per cent and robberies by 26 per cent. Police recruitment was in a critical state. The number of officers resigning each year had risen by 60 per cent since Labour came to power. As the *Daily Telegraph* commented:"Anybody who believes that none of this has anything to do with the Macpherson report wants his head examining." And went on to suggest a campaign slogan for the Tories: "Less PC, more Pcs." (*Daily Telegraph* 15.12.2000.)

But now let's look at a few instances in the wider community, in which Macpherson claimed to find extensive institutional racism, of the disruptive effects of his report and the stimulus it gave to the racial heresy-hunting psychosis which it bred.

Firemen in hot water

In September '99 the firemen were in triple trouble, being condemned in a report of the Fire Service Inspectorate, as not only racist but as sexist and homophobic (PC-speak for homosexual) as well. Their "Macho and laddish culture" was said to be due to the "Watch" system under which officers could work for years in the same group, developing a family-like closeness. The Home Office Minister Mike O'Brien said that the report showed there was a stark contrast between the high standards with which the service carried out its, often dangerous, work and its internal culture. Of course nobody dared suggest that, for all its faults, the internal culture, including the family closeness, might have a good deal to do with their capacity to work as a team and therefore with the high standards with which they carried out their hazardous tasks

Bar Stool Cronyism

Come November '99 Jack Straw, in response to complaints, was tut-tutting about how Asian women missed out on job promotion in the Home Office because they did not go for a drink after work to the pub, where vacancies and career advancement were often discussed largely by white males.

On the same occasion he also set targets for ethnic prison officers' recruitment, retention and promotion (not, mercifully, related to the ethnic breakdown of the prison population).

Barristers in the dock

Next it was the turn of the lawyers. The Bar Council produced a plan to eradicate institutional racism at the Bar, which proposed that the selection of judges and Queen's Council could be made subject to anti-discrimination laws. The recommendations included racial awareness training for all barristers, ethnic monitoring, provision for grievances about discrimination by heads of chambers or colleagues to be brought before employment tribunals.(*Times* 11.12.99.)

One month later, the Crown Prosecution Service was arraigned and given three months to tackle racism after complaints about bias were upheld. By June Home Office Minister, Paul Boateng, on the basis of yet another report, was accusing the Probation Service of being "infected" with racism to quite an unacceptable degree.

Sins of the C of E

Days afterwards, a report commissioned by the Southwark diocese and chaired by Sir Herman Ouseley, then head of the Commission for Racial Equality, found (surprise! surprise!) that institutional racism was rife in the Church of England, due to an "imperial and colonial mentality".

It is fitting to conclude this brief selection of examples, from Macpherson up to the end of the millennium year, of what became a progressive anti-racist witch-hunt by turning to the demand during the Christmas season from the *Mirror* newspaper (the chief media cheer-leader for the Blair government) that there should be a government inquiry into why the popular quiz programme, *Who Wants*

To Be a Millionaire?, only featured 1.6% black faces, or why The Generation Game, Catchphrase and Wheel had no ethnic minority contestants at all! Hands up anyone who can say what the CRE's answer to this million-dollar question would be?

Law Society Condemned

A more recent example of the way the Macpherson virus is infecting our institutions was the finding of an employment tribunal that the secretary-general of the Law Society, the solicitors' ruling body, had discriminated against Kamlesh Bahl, its former vice-president, on racial and sexual grounds. She had been obliged to resign allegedly because she had harassed and bullied staff. The tribunal found that she was treated less favourably than a white man would have been in the same situation. Yet the allegation of bullying had in fact been fully investigated by Lord Griffiths, a former Law Lord, who found that Miss Bahl's treatment of staff was "at times demeaning and humiliating and at other times offensively aggressive". Despite this the tribunal found in her favour, even though it also admitted that she told whopping lies to it while under oath. How in these circumstances could the tribunal have reached such a decision? The only plausible explanation is that it was abiding by the preposterous Macpherson definition of a racist action as one which is described as such by the victim.

What all these examples show is that the CRE's witch-hunt is prospering. Partly by stealth, but now more and more openly, whole sections of our society are bullied into mouthing the catechism that British society is racist and must pay penance for it by affirmative action, that is guaranteeing privileged treatment for ethnic minorities. More than that, the indigenous majority is supposed, not to take pride in its history, but to hang its head in shame.

Erasing British identity

This was the message of the report in October 2000 — and a strange one to come from a body which rejoices in the name of The Runnymede Trust — on *The Future of Multi-cultural Britain*. It portrayed Britishness as "racist" and called for a "reworking" of British history. The vice-chairman of the commission that produced the report, Lady Gavron, apparently one of Tony Blair's intimate circle of friends, told a *Daily Telegraph* reporter that Prince Charles should have married a black woman as a symbol of his support for multicultural Britain. She felt that the Royal Family should take a lead in promoting racial integration, not because she had any time for its members — "We don't need them, but they're fun for the tourists to look at" was how she breezily dismissed them — but, presumably to help persuade what she regards as the dumb multitude who still admire them to adopt the anti-racist agenda. She further opined that the word "English" was far more danger-ous than "British!". "English is much more racially coded. The word summons up images of football hooliganism and white Essex men".

Jack Straw's u-turn

The real attitude of New Labour is indeed better revealed by such of its sillier acolytes than by its official spin doctors, whose statements were rushed out as soon as it was realised in Number 10 how unpopular the Runnymede Trust report's attack on the British had proved. Jack Straw, whose Home Office had welcomed the report when it was issued as "a timely contribution" to the debate on race relations, did a nimble u-turn and attacked the political (and by implication unpatriotic) Left, well represented on the Commission for "washing its hands of the whole notion of nationhood". He went on to announce that he was proud to be British. Tony

Blair's spokesman followed up with a comment so fatuous that one could only assume that he must have had rather a good lunch: "Britishness to us is about issues as varied as how you manage the economy, the approach you take to issues like unemployment, your vision of society."

The giveaway

Yet it was Lady Gavron who gave authentic expression to her party leadership's scorn for our institutions. These include not only the monarchy, which of course it would like to remove just as it already has removed the hereditary peers, but also the House of Commons, which it is busy making into a poodle assembly, along with the ordinary citizen's historic common law rights — habeas corpus, trial by jury, the principle that the accused is innocent until proved guilty — which it is intent on whittling away. It is now becoming clear that New Labour, insofar as it stands for anything other than opportunism, is increasingly identified with a political correctness crusade, which aims to foster collective demands, mainly with regard to race, sex and culture. These are propagated under the heading of equal opportunities, but their object is the very opposite — to promote group privileges at everyone else's expense. Individual rights as understood by Locke, Mill, Hume and other traditional liberal thinkers were a private realm, sacrosanct to the individual, where government entry was banned. Such rights limited state power. The rights of the PC agenda, by contrast, are group claims, enforced by government at everyone else's expense. These magnify state power and diminish the individual.

PC and anti-British

For all their claims to novelty, New Labour is at one with the party's tradition — in its belief first in the boundless redemptive power of political action and second in the moral superiority of those who share their faith. However, when the old gang tried to redeem the economy through nationalisation, it proved a huge flop and a vote-losing flop too, especially when harnessed with union smash and grab. It was not penitence and humble acknowledgement of error but yearning for office that transformed Labour from the party of unlimited public ownership, into the even more morally self-righteous (but actually venal — ask the Hinduja brothers) party of political correctness. Clearly anti-racism is a major part of this agenda. Its exponents play a key role in New Labour's assault on our traditional institutions by decrying our nation's history and seeking to destroy pride in our past. Of course, when they are put on the spot, they deny doing any such thing. Thus Lord Parekh, Chairman of the Runnymede Commission on Multi-Ethnic Britain in an article in the *Daily Telegraph* (18.10.00) said: "Let me begin by saying what the report does not say. It neither claims nor in the slightest way implies that the word British is racist." Yet the tone of the actual report is quite at odds with this disclaimer. There is for instance a passage about the "systematic racial connotations" of the word "Britishness". And how else but as an accusation of racism can we interpret the following pronouncement? — "The Brits do appear to believe that Britons never, never shall be slaves...(but) it is impossible to colonise three-fifths of the world with unspeakable barbarism, occasioning several holocausts in the process, without enslaving oneself in the process".

A saner view

Contrast this paranoid rant with the sober judgment of a distinguished Australian historian, Keith Windschuttle, who, in an article in the *New Criterion* (quoted by Norman Podhoretz in *Commentary* (January 2000) wrote:

British imperial rule in many parts of Asia, Africa and the

> Americas, while it may not have been representative or
> democratic, was nonetheless orderly, largely benign and
> usually fair. For all their faults, most British colonial offi-
> cials delivered good government — or at least better gov-
> ernment than any of the likely alternatives."

Nor, economically, was the British Empire a mere exercise
in exploitation as the Marxists and the rest of the Left have
portrayed it. Admittedly the British did engage in the slave
trade. That was a stain on the reputation of all involved.
Yet that roster of the guilty should include the African kings
and chieftains who sold their countrymen into slavery. True,
they may not have appreciated the cruel fate which awaited
the victims, of being overworked by their European masters, but many of the vendors apparently thought it would
be crueller still — they believed that slaves would be eaten.
(Review by John Carey of 1688, A Global History , by
John E. Wills, *Sunday Times* Culture supplement 18.2.01).
On the other side of the account, it should be recalled, it
was the British parliament, which emancipated slaves
throughout the British Empire, at considerable cost to the
taxpayer, (preceding the USA and other countries by decades) and the Royal Navy, which patrolled the high seas
thereafter to stop the traffic. Again, as that doyen of development economists, Lord Bauer, never tired of pointing
out, the British did not take rubber out of Malaya but introduced it to a place where no such plants had ever existed
before. And so it was with other resources in other colonies.

   This assault on national self-esteem, however, continues
apace among left wing ideologues and is of a piece with
the revisionism of two New Labour historians of the
"collaborationist" school, Linda Colley and Norman
Davies, who claim that the idea of Britishness is an artificial
construct. (What a contrast with the dictum of that fine
historian, the late H.A.L. Fisher: "England grew: Prussia

was manufactured".) They think that our nation is an accidental by-product of Protestantism and external threats exploited by a ruling élite. They argue that since Protestantism, the external threats and the old ruling class are as good as done for, the British nation state is dead and there is nothing to stop us rushing into the arms of the European superstate.

Decrying Britain

This perspective suits Europhile Tony Blair admirably. In this respect he belongs to a long anti-British tradition on the Labour Left, of whom George Orwell once remarked, that they were inverted patriots whose first loyalty was to Moscow. For "Moscow", today, read "Brussels", which not only poses a threat to British interests, sovereignty and liberties, but has the inestimable merit, in Left-wing eyes, of favouring the growth of trade union power. As the historian Andrew Roberts commented "Blair is embarrassed by Britain's past and dislikes the way our history teaches Britons the off-message truth about our country, which is that historically, we have done very well being in Europe but not run by it." It is significant that this Government of reluctant Brits had no plans to celebrate the Act of Union which took place two hundred years ago, though, of course, the British have been around much longer than that because they have had the same monarch for twice as long. The reality is that the Britain is an old and great country. Its people know it and rejoice in the fact.

Multicultural poppycock

It was predictable that Lord Parekh should demand, in a *Daily Telegraph* article just after the publication of the Runnymede report, an official declaration that Britain is a multicultural society. Yet, as international lawyer Torquil Dick-Ericsson responded in the letter column, Lord Parekh failed to distinguish between "multi-ethnic" and "multicultural". As he pointed out, " Ethnicity, or racial origin, is a matter of skin colour and physical appearance. Culture is a matter of values and social practices. ...the British are tolerant of other cultures. We adopt some aspects of them, such as cuisine or music, with enthusiasm. But we cannot respect values which do not respect our basic human liberties — for example, forced marriages or genital mutilation".

It is absurd to insist, as the multiculturalists usually do, that all cultures are of equal value. Other cultures deserve generally to be treated with respect, but not in absolutely every case or without qualification. Would any of our multiculturalists support the claims of a cannibal culture, a Nazi culture or the culture involving suttee, the practice of a 19th century Indian sect of burning widows on their late husband's funeral pyre?

The one and only sense in which it is sensible to call Britain a multicultural society, (apart from the trivial observation that numerous cultures exist in Britain), is, insofar as the content of each different culture is lawful. The unifying factor is the law, which applies to everyone and applies to everyone in the same way, Yet, this is precisely what the multiculturalists do not accept. They want the law to apply differently to racial minorities to give them privileged access to jobs, promotion, education and housing through affirmative action.

Identifying race with culture is playing a dangerous game, the game of the real racists. As the philosopher and logician, Professor Antony Flew, neatly put it:

> Those who ...constantly confound race with culture need to be reminded that it was an essential element in the authentically racist teachings of Adolf Hitler's National-Socialist Workers' Party that German high culture could not have been produced and could not be fully shared by

anyone not of the right, supposedly superior race.

Multiethnic not Multicultural

The best description of the position is that, like the Roman Empire, Britain is a multi-ethnic but not, except in the limited sense of belonging to the same jurisdiction, a multicultural society, nor is there any good reason why it should be — certainly not for the benefit of those who have immigrated here. Indeed nothing could be more lethal to the economic and social prospects of ethnic immigrants than enforcing policies under the rubric of "multiculturalism", which push them into the ghetto by denying them the opportunity to share in British cultural life and its magnificent inheritance. The argument that culture is the supremely important unifying influence in society unimpeded by so-called biological racial differences, is reinforced by the recent successful completion by scientists of the analysis of the human genome. This shows that people from different racial groups can be more genetically similar than individuals in the same group. As Dr Craig Venter, of Celera Genomics, the research team leader, remarked: "No serious scholar in this field thinks that race is a scientific concept." (*Daily Telegraph* 12.2.01.) The implication is clear: culture — meaning language, literature, ways of thinking, academic and everyday, aesthetic and scientific, music, manners, skills, laws, moral attitudes, customs and traditions of behaviour — is overwhelmingly the crucial factor in what we call "race". Cultures can be learnt and enjoyed by people of all types and origins and, when learnt and enjoyed, provide the basis of social harmony and successful democracy. There is no contradiction in individuals or groups successfully belonging to a minority as well as the mainstream British culture. However multiculturalism, interpreted by the race relations industry as the deliberate disintegration of the mainstream culture of our country and the granting of equal status of all cultures defined by racial groupings, is a recipe for social and racial strife. Multiculturalism equals ghettoism.

European threat

It is intriguing to note that Torquil Dick-Ericsson, referred to earlier, was the first person to warn of the European Commission's scheme to unify by stealth the legal structures of the EU countries in the so-called Corpus Juris, which would threaten habeas corpus, trial by jury and the presumption of innocence of the accused until proved guilty. The Amsterdam Treaty moved this process forward, allowing the European Commission to issue directives to stamp on discrimination, not only on race, but on sex, religion, disability, age or sexual orientation. As Melanie Philips pointed out (*Sunday Times* 4.6.00) the fundamental principle of English law — that everything is permitted unless it is expressly forbidden is giving way to the reverse (continental) principle that nothing is permitted unless it is expressly allowed. On present trends it looks as if the CRE will soon realize its long-held ambition of changing the law so that those accused of racism will be presumed guilty until they prove themselves innocent. If Westminster does not do it, Brussels will. Indeed the EU has already established, in 1999, a busybody institution in Vienna called the Monitoring Centre on Racism and Xenophobia. As with so many of the European Union bodies, it is inefficiently run and has now been reprimanded by the Court of Auditors for of its dodgy accounts. The reaction of Left-wing MEPs was shock! horror! at anyone daring to find fault with it and they proceeded to question the critics' motives. As Tory MEP, Daniel Hannan, put it: "It seems that to criticise the Monitoring Centre on Racism and Xenophobia — even for lack of financial rectitude — is itself evidence of racism and xenophobia." (*Sunday Telegraph*

18.2.01.) This was precisely the same style of accusation as that which Macpherson levelled against members of the Metropolitan Police who disputed his opinion that they were unwittingly racist, or which the heresy-hunting inquisitors of the past used to silence and even to charge, arrest and burn their critics.

Growing immigration

The need to question the wholesale remodelling of our institutions in the name of multiculturalism is all the more urgent in view of the rising tide of immigration. A Home Office research report published in January 2001 said that immigration was likely to continue at "historically high levels" reaching almost 180,000 a year by 2005, compared with 40,000 in 1985 and 70,000 only six years earlier. The main reasons for this growth were the growth of the City of London, labour mobility in the EU and asylum seekers. The forecast seems likely to be an underestimate. It was already 185,000 in 1999 — almost the size of a London borough — and no-one really knows how many illegal immigrants there are. David Coleman, Reader in Demography in Oxford suggested in *The Spectator"* (6.1.01) that it is quite possible that the present white majority will become a minority by the end of the century. Some greet this as good news, arguing that the newcomers will shoulder the problem of an ageing population and the declining proportion of the population of working age. This sanguine belief, he points out sharply, is nonsense. Britain has no demographic crisis — though the same cannot be said for our neighbours in the EU, where the population replacement rate is much lower and which, in most cases, will not be able to fund their national pension promises by the middle of the century. The ageing of our population is a perfectly natural consequence of lower death rates and family planning. As Coleman says, "Sensible adjustments of workforce participation, retirement age and pension funding should manage this." On the other hand, he adds, in order to preserve the present ratio of taxpayers to pensioners for the next 50 years would require immigration at the rate of a million a year, doubling the population to 120 million. This cannot be treated as an acceptable prospect.

Setting limits

Like many others he fears that, if we are not to lose our identity, there must be radical curbs on immigration. That is a logical deduction if we continue with the Runnymede Trust agenda, already largely in place, of deliberately changing our identity, through modifying our educational system, reinventing our history, imposing a culture of apology, intrusive ethnic monitoring and distortion of long-established legal principles meant to protect personal freedom.

The alternative is to combine a properly thought out, more relaxed immigration policy with a rejection of multiculturalism lock, stock and barrel. Multiculturalism (not, I repeat, to be confused with multi-ethnicism), far from being a solution to the problems of immigration, can only aggravate them. In matters of race, equality of opportunity must again be made to mean in practice what it originally meant — treating everybody equally. Ultimately, colour is not important. There are already plenty of black and Asian people who are as British and feel themselves to be as British as any Lambeth Cockney or Dorset farmer. However it normally takes a generation or two for immigrants to feel this way. Apparently youthful Britons of Paakistani origin still fail Norman Tebbit's cricket test — do they cheer for the British eleven? — at least when Britain is playing Pakistan. It also takes time for the host community to accept the newcomers and here the numbers are the key factor, as critics, from Enoch Powell on, have insisted. There is no compelling reason why we should not take in as many immigrants as we, as a society, can comfortably absorb. Fortunately, there is no doubt that attitudes among the majority population towards coloured immigrants have changed decisively and positively from the time when we were an imperial power.

Benefits of immigration

What is crucial for future racial harmony is that immigrants be prepared to accept the laws and customs of this country and that they should not seek or receive special treatment for themselves or for their communities of the same ethnic origin. Given that approach, British national culture is resilient and adaptable enough to allow for a relatively liberal attitude to immigration. There would also be economic benefits in terms of growth and competitiveness such as the US has enjoyed. But to obtain this happy result we need to have as much faith in the ability of our free institutions to work for newcomers as the Americans. Such faith will be only be justified if we stop wrecking or dismantling those institutions ourselves out of a misplaced sense of guilt. Admittedly, as I have pointed out earlier, the Americans have, in recent times, originated some particularly wrongheaded policies on racial matters, which have served as a disastrous model for so-called reformers in Britain. Even so, we should not lose sight of the bigger picture. What really demands our admiration is their long-term achievement of taking in huge numbers of immigrants and absorbing them into the American way of life, while still preserving and indeed strengthening their free institutions (the French intellectuals now on their fifth republic who sneer at what they regard as American stupidity born of the immaturity of a "young" nation should instead be envying the sound institutions and the popular commonsense which have made the USA the oldest as well as the most democratic republic in the world).

Policy to suit our needs

Of course as long as we have our present kind of welfare state, a laissez-faire attitude towards immigration is not practicable, though the Labour peer, Lord Desai has suggested that there should be unlimited immigration on condition that those who come in should not be entitled to any welfare benefits. Although this is a logical position, it would have to face up to the possibility of people starving or dying of disease for lack of treatment, which seems to me to call for an unrealistic degree of hard-heartedness among the general public. What is required, surely, is an immigration policy, which is deliberately and unabashedly related to national economic needs. There are three types of economically desirable immigrants: those with skills which Britain requires, the unskilled who are prepared to do work for which it is hard to recruit from the existing population and those with capital which creates jobs for others. It is not feasible, however, to put such an immigration policy into effect without tackling the asylum crisis. In 2001 Britain took more asylum seekers than any other European country and this must have something to do with the fact that there is, and continues to be, no effective control over those who come here. It is ridiculous to describe as an immigration policy a system, which allows so many who have been refused to slip through the net. Most asylum seekers are economic migrants, almost 90 per cent of them have their applications rejected, but, at least until recently, only a risible proportion of them have been deported and it can reasonably be assumed that most of them have stayed on illegally. The Labour government claimed to be addressing the problem by increasing the number of officials dealing with applications at the ports, but the impression that this was only tinkering with the problem was confirmed only a fortnight later when the Immigration Service Union stated that the government's figure of 9,000 immigrants returned out of the 76,000 rejected in the year 2000, bad though it was, seriously overestimated the numbers sent back. This was because the official tally did not distinguish between voluntary and forced removals. Union spokesman, John Tinsey, said that those asylum-seekers who leave are the ones who are happy to accept a free ticket, while barely any are expelled against their will. He told BBC Radio: "I would be very surprised if we are actually removing 12 people a month who don't want to go home. We really don't have a working method at the moment for removing people who don't want to go home." The *Daily Telegraph* in an editorial (1.2.01) spelt out what needed to be done.

> Only when the Government summons up the courage to stop asylum seekers at the ports, deal with them there and (preferably) then and there send back those who fail, will it have any hope of turning the problem round. Of that, as yet, there is no sign at all.

Much Spin: No Action

It may have been this comment, which prompted the Government to brief reporters that, in response to the large numbers of refugees arriving at the Kent ports, it aimed to deport them pronto. Prime Minister Blair was said to be preparing to press President Chirac at an Anglo-French summit (on February 9th 2001) for French support for this plan. In the event Chirac was far from ecstatic: he had refugee problems of his own. In any case, whatever the attitude of the French, summarily whisking new arrivals back across the Channel was not on: the Law Lords had ruled such action unlawful only a few weeks before. Following hard on his leader's heels, Home Secretary Jack Straw called for a revision of the UN convention on refugees (which obliges countries to offer sanctuary to people who claim "a well-founded fear of persecution"). As he said, "Everybody has to recognise that the system has drifted out of the control of governments into the hands of criminal gangs." (*Daily Telegraph* 7.2.01.) The trouble with this sort of talk is that it tends to make all immigrants sound like criminals. Yet legal immigration is not a crime. If criminal gangs are targeting Britain as the most suitable country for smuggling immigrants, it is precisely because of the shambles of our immigration control, which has allowed nine out of ten of those who land here claiming asylum to stay, so that Britain is, naturally enough, considered to be a soft touch. However, Straw's call for a revision of the UN Convention was even more unrealistic than the Blair proposal, as more than 100 countries are signatory to it and revision would take years. Both pronouncements seemed to be no more than just further exercises in the sound bites and spin-doctoring which the Blair government so often resorts to when it hasn't a clue what to do next. What was lacking was political will. A *Daily Telegraph* leader (7.2.01) summed up the position succinctly:

> If the UN Convention is the problem, and it is certainly part of it, then the answer is to replace it with a domestic law of our own devising.

Home Office Moves

Stung by these criticisms and conscious of an election approaching and the opinion polls showing that immigration and asylum matters were among the few on which the Tories scored better with the public than Labour, the Home Office produced a number of initiatives. A Refugee Community Development Fund was launched to assist small community-based groups in their work with refugees. On asylum it announced a programme to return 30,000 failed asylum-seekers and 700 new immigration officers to do this work and reinforce controls. It also announced an intention to encourage voluntary returns at the end of the asylum process. In addition there were to be 1,800 new detention spaces, a specialist anti-trafficking unit, cooperation with French authorities, introduction of a fully-automated finger-printing system, faster turnround of asylum-seekers, an effort to reform the Dublin Convention (covering applications within the European Union), extending the existing civil penalty on road hauliers bringing in illegal immigrants to rail traffic, over 500 new asylum decision-makers and a doubling of the number of courtrooms at the Immigration Appellate Authority. This certainly appeared more businesslike, and it claimed that the number of outstanding asylum application had just halved. Yet the promise of more cooperation with the French authorities — not very helpful so far, as we have seen, — and the proposal to revise the Dublin Convention, which would require unanimous agreement of all the other signatories, looked suspect to say the least. As for the statistics of asylum-seekers dealt with, as the *Economist* put it (18.8.2001) "the proportion of people permitted to stay is much higher than the headline figures imply".

While Labour made a last-minute effort to redeem itself before the General Election from its drift on immigration and asylum matters, the Conservatives, who started from a strong position in the public eye, were let down by the unconvincing policy produced by their abrasive spokesman, Ann Widdecombe (who had earlier reversed the Conservative revival in the polls at the time of the lorry-drivers' protest with her scheme for dire penalties for anyone found possessing cannabis). Her plan to lock up all asylum-seekers in secure reception centres, in effect jailing thousands of innocent people, many of them torture victims, did not appeal to the electors either,though that is precisely the direction in which Labour policy found itself heading once the election was over.

Cherry-picking?

On immigration matters we could do worse than take our cue from the Continent. Germany is already contemplating a policy based on national economic priorities. Gerhard Schroder, the German Chancellor has proposed to let in up to 20,000 Indian computer scientists. Pursuing the same line of thought, in February 2001 Romano Prodi, President of the European Commission called for the immigration of hundreds of thousands of overseas workers with information skills, which are badly-needed. He stressed that bringing in qualified immigrants was quite different from mass immigration. "Genuinely-skilled labour immigration doesn't cause problems from an economic or social point of view", he said. This approach is criticised by some as cherry-picking by advanced countries of the skilled workers which Third World countries need for their own development. In fact their home countries are likely to benefit from money sent back to relatives, and some who prosper may return taking back useful practical knowledge with them. Besides, many of the jobs which are available here often either are hard to find or don't even exist in their homelands.

A welcoming rather than a grudging attitude to immigration would surely pay. As the Home Office study showed, Britain's foreign-born population contributes an estimated 10 per cent more into the Treasury than it takes out. This is because migrants, on average earn more than the rest of the existing population but do not claim more than their share of benefits.

Control Essential

To repeat, what's called for is an immigration policy to

suit the country's needs. This could also be a comparatively liberal one, but only on condition that we stem the flow of illegals, who are either smuggled in, or, after being officially rejected, one way or another manage to remain. For it stands to reason that, given there has to be some limit on the numbers permitted to come in, the more who manage to slip in illegally, the greater the pressure to restrict the numbers who *are* acceptable. The corollary also holds: the fewer who enter the country illegally, the less restrictive we can afford to be towards those who would qualify on either asylum or economic grounds. The newcomers will only be successfully integrated into our society, however, if they do not receive special privileges but are treated as full citizens on the same basis as everybody else. The implication of such a policy is that the anti-racist apparatus of law and administration could then be dismantled. This proposition, or something like it, is supported in many, often surprising, quarters. For example Yasmin Alibhai-Brown in her book *After Multiculturalism* published by the independent but progressive think-tank, the Foreign Policy Centre, says, "…we need to ensure that valuing diversity is seen to be about enabling everybody to succeed, not special treatment for favoured minorities".

It is intriguing that Ms Alibhai-Brown, who obviously understands the dangers of the policy of favouring minorities, wants to get rid of the Commission for Racial Equality — which stands above all else for such a policy — as well as the Equal Opportunities Commission and have a single body — a Human Rights Commission — for all areas of citizenship. This is welcome insofar as it indicates an impatience with the inadequacy of the CRE in some places where one would expect it to command unqualified support. However to replace it with an all-encompassing Human Rights Commission would be a case of diving out of the frying pan of institutionalised anti-racism into a scorching PC fire. For such a body could become a Star Chamber for rooting out and punishing all who offend against the doctrines of political correctness. Thus the fact that the Lord Chancellor, Lord Irvine, has adopted the idea of removing the CRE and EOC might at first blush appear encouraging, until we learn that he too wants their work taken over by a Human Rights Commission with sub-divisions reflecting the existing commissions. So, far from disappearing, they would become more menacing by merging into a more powerful monster, all, no doubt, in aid of a master plan to move Britain towards a "rights-based culture" (*Daily Telegraph* 23.3.01).

The perils of this approach were perceptively summed up by *Sunday Times*' columnist Melanie Phillips. "We need a rights-based culture like we need a hole in the head. A rights culture creates a culture of litigious complaint, manu-factures rival interest groups of victims and fosters not co-operation but tribalism." As she points out, for every right there is a competing right — a right to live versus a right of the suffering to die, for example. Which right should take priority is likely to be highly subjective. The result is that what we are confronted with is not rights at all but power. Thus, as she says, "The basis of English liberty under which everything is allowed unless specifically prohibited is to be replaced by a coercive, oppressive culture in which the only things that are permitted are those laid down by the courts and enforced through a centralised bureaucracy." (*Sunday Times* 25.3.2001) and for "courts" read "judges", a multiplicity of Macphersons, personally worthy enough no doubt, but, inevitably reflecting the fashionable PC ide-ology.

What a long way we have travelled from John Locke's concept of liberty under the law, where "the laws are known and certain" and a citizen shall not be "subject to the in-constant, uncertain, unknown, arbitrary will of another man" (John Locke, *Second Treatise on Civil Government*, Blackwell 1948.)

This rights, or victim, culture was invented in the United States, which has created the phenomenon of "hate crime", applied to offenders guilty of prejudice against people on grounds of race, gender or sexual orientation, and has created a nastily polarised society. In the wake of the Macpherson Report, hate crime has now arrived in Britain, though, as many an editorial has pointed out, this seems more a job for the thought police than for the British bobbies. However it has been made a "ministerial priority" according to Glen Smyth , chairman of the Metropolitan Police Federation. In pursuit of this priority on 30 March 2001, 20 officers of the Metropolitan Police in what has come to be called the "curry patrol" or "Balti-house beat" sallied forth to Indian, Chinese and Thai restaurants to spy on diners and note if they were racially offensive to waiters. This was not a one-off. A similar expedition, known as "Operation Napkin" was launched in the millennium year with curry patrols continuing for seven weeks in Gloucestershire. This resulted in one caution and one prosecution, which was thrown out because of procedural irregularities (Focus Report by Richard Woods and Rosie Waterhouse, *Sunday Times* 1.4.2001). Such is the priority imposed on our police, who are critically short of officers, at a time when violent crimes have reached a new peak.

Oldham Riots

To make things worse riots and fights between white and Asian youths broke out in Bradford and more seriously in Oldham in April and May 2001 with bricks and petrol bombs and assaults on the police. Predictably these were attributed to the racism of British society. As the Oldham riots happened during the 2001 General Election the opportunity was seized by Liberal Democrat Simon Hughes to put the blame for them on the Tories, suggesting that William Hague's remarks about asylum-seekers had inflamed tempers and made the riots worse. It is true that Hague had made a speech talking about the danger of Britain's native population feeling in future that they were in a foreign land, but this was a reference to the growing interference in our affairs from Brussels, which, he believed was threatening our democracy and imposing laws we did not want. Hughes was, on this occasion, put in his place by Jack Straw, who pooh-poohed the idea that the riots had anything to do with Hague. They also had nothing to do with racism, as Manzoor Moghal, a Labour chairman of Moslem organisations in Leicester and a Labour Party member, stated in an article in the *Daily Mail* (29 May 2001). As he said "the reality is that Oldham was a powder keg waiting to blow, not because of racial tensions but because it is an area of poverty, deprivation and sheer desperation for too many of its inhabitants. Housing is substandard, education is inadequate and unemployment running at 35 to 40 per cent." Oldham is a rundown area because most of the textile factories, which provided the bulk of the employment there, have gone out of business. However, while not the ultimate cause of the troubles, racism was a factor, though not in the way the race relations lobby like to suggest. Oldham was targeted by racial extremists and the presumption is they got a response from poor, white, uneducated youths who felt that they were losing out because of an official policy giving privileges to minority ethnic groups. This is not mere speculation. A report by Greenwich council and the Institute of Education in the wake of the Stephen Lawrence murder said that white racist attitudes sprang from a pronounced feeling of unfairness that their interests were ignored by the authorities and the media. Pronouncements by Robin Cook and others about the lack of English identity and about Britain being a multicultural country are a godsend to the British National Party and the National Front. At the same time the assertion by those in authority that there is no mainstream culture and that all cultures are of equal status, robs the young Asians of the ladder up which former immigrants, like the Jews, climbed out of the ghetto and achieved prosperity and fulfilment. The only assimilation the Asian youths of Oldham seem have achieved in the wider community has been with the thuggish behaviour of some of our white teenagers. Further, if these Asian youths, who derived from a notably peaceful culture, now, in their newly-adopted yobbish persona choose to attack the police, is that so surprising after the Macpherson report which labelled all our police forces racist? Meanwhile, as Melanie Phillips, with her usual incisiveness put it: "the manifest injustice of that report's blanket denunciation has caused resentful officers to dismiss any protests over race as just another politically-motivated whinge. So misunderstandings bubble along until boiling point is reached." (*Sunday Times* 2.6.01. "Race Riots Grow out of the Balkanisation of Britain" by Melanie Phillips).

White Backlash

Worse still the Macpherson report has produced a "White Backlash" leading to a rise in racial violence and harassment which reaches beyond Oldham. This is the conclusion of a leading authority on race relations, Dr Marion Fitzgerald, who has accused the Macpherson report of being "hugely divisive". Her analysis of studies of actual and potential perpetrators of racial violence and harassment show that many come from marginalised groups in the white population. As she says, "As justification for their activities they draw heavily on perceptions of preferential treatment of minorities". Moreover, she claimed, by concentrating on the way the criminal justice system dealt with ethnic minorities the Government was undermining its parallel drive to cut crime and disorder and lift confidence in the system in the whole community. She warned against projects which "racialised" problems. Such, of course, have been many of the projects, like the anti-hate campaigns of the CRE and some of our police forces, referred to above, which hunt, or rather witch hunt for a racial element in crime and conflict in our inner cities, which are however primarily linked to family and community breakdown, poverty and ignorance. (*Daily Telegraph* 2.6.01.)

As if to confirm Marion Fitzgerald's findings, the election results in the two Oldham parliamentary constituencies showed a substantial vote for the normally insignificant British National Party. In Oldham East and Saddleworth the BNP got 11.2 per cent of the total vote; in Oldham West and Royton, Michael Meacher's seat, 16.4 per cent.

More Riots

Worse was to come. On Saturday afternoon July 7, 2001, about 500 people, mostly young Asians, gathered in Bradford's Centenary Square for an anti-Nazi League demonstration to protest at a threatened rally by the National Front which did not in fact materialise. Trouble flared after a group of white men who had been drinking in a pub confronted Asian youths and shouted racial insults. Violence erupted in which hundreds of Asian and some white youths attacked and fought running battles with 1000 police in riot gear, throwing stones, fireworks and petrol bombs. A Labour and a Conservative club were set alight and white-owned businesses targeted. Two days later a white gang staged revenge attacks on Asian businesses. However, much of the damage seems to have been indiscriminate and to deserve the description "mindless". The violence was prolonged because of the "cautious" approach of the police who would have done better to resort immediately to water cannon and tear gas. But then who could blame them for being reluctant to take the necessary tough action when their predictable reward would be a barrage of accusations of racism? The superficial interpretation of these events was that it was all started by the National Front, but there were less than a score of them in Bradford on the day of the riot and, as Sion Simon, Labour MP for Birmingham, Erdington, pointed out in an article in the *Daily Telegraph* (9.7.01) the most effective agents provocateurs were the Revolutionary Trotskyist Left, who were moving spirits in the Anti-Nazi League. The Prime Minister's dismissal of the riots as thuggery requiring a law and order response was pretty near the mark. Certainly there were complicating factors, drugs played their part as well as machismo, not to mention criminal gangs seeking opportunities for creating mayhem and acquiring loot.

What was intended to be a more measured pronouncement came from a team led by Lord Ouseley, former hcairman of the CRE. Their report identified as the main problems:

- The inability to talk openly about problems across cultural communities without fear of recrimination or to challenge wrongdoing.

- Polarisation of young people along racial, ethnic and religious lines and the "virtual apartheid" in secondary schools.

- An irrational fear of Islam among the non-Muslim population.

- Fear among the police of being labelled racist and having their prospects damaged if they tackled black and Asian offenders.

The intriguing aspect of this report is the extent to which it parallels the analysis put forward by former Headmaster, Ray Honeyford, in the article in the *Salisbury Review* fifteen years before, which caused him to be shamefully persecuted by the Bradford City educational authorities as well as mercilessly pilloried by the race relations industry. It is heartening, if also ironic, to find Lord Ouseley expatiating on some of the above popular fears. After all who should be held responsible for the inability to talk openly about racial matters, or the fear of the police of dealing with Asian offenders if not the CRE and its minions, not to mention its brother-in-arms Macpherson with his blanket condemnation of the endemic racism he claimed to find both in the police and in the whole of British society? Lord Ouseley's call for education in citizenship in schools and for young people to learn about the diversity of the local community is welcome. Yet the CRE, from whose direction he has so recently taken leave, has long aspired to have control of the school curriculum. If his successors in the CRE have their way, the content of every school subject will be drenched in anti-racist propaganda and all teachers subjected to unrelenting instruction in racial awareness.

In Sum

All of the above — and not least the view now held by Lord Ouseley — points to one over-arching conclusion: the counter-productive effect of government action in race relations. That has been the pervading theme of this study. I have tried to demonstrate that the record of attempts by government to combat racism proves that it is not the right institution to perform this task. Of course this conclusion runs contrary to the widespread, seemingly ineradicable, belief that politics provides a pill for every ill — the worst and most enduring legacy of Marxism in Britain. It is curious that this faith in the unlimited potential of political action, which strangely coincides with a declining respect for politicians and an ever-lower turnout of voters in General Elections, survives intact, despite its miserable record in managing industry. For nationalisation, not only in Communist countries but in western democracies as well, has been an abject failure. Yet this naïve attachment to statism prospers alongside an equally dangerous illusion introduced by television documentaries, which give the impression that even the most intractable of human problems can be solved in a half- hour programme. The Blair government, for all its revisionism has evidently not learned this lesson but promises to compound past errors by initiating further state action in the area of race relations. Its General Election manifesto undertook to implement the recommendations of the egregious Macpherson report including the 'reform', as it called it, of the 'double jeopardy' law for murder. In the Queen's speech it proved as good as its word in its proposals for criminal justice reforms in which it proposed to introduce not only 'double jeopardy' in murder cases but a number of other curbs on ancient liberties including a limit on right to trial by jury and an erosion of the principle of 'innocent until proved guilty'. It is curious that this government, which has, for all practical purposes recognised that the nationalisation formula has been such a flop when applied to industry, should expect it to be any better when applied to race. We would do better to rely on free enterprise in good neighbourliness for creating good relations between different ethnic groups within a framework of law which is equal for all citizens and on the good nature and commonsense of the British people. Ethnic minorities would do better to put their faith not in government favours but in a law under which they enjoy full equality and which is put into effect by a colour-neutral police force. Admittedly the adjustment will take time, but all the signs are that, in the new generation of native Brits, the prejudices of their parents have largely disappeared.

The process which enabled large numbers of Flemings, French Huguenots, Irish, Jews and Poles, to mention but a few, to be successfully assimilated over time is continuing in the case of West Indians, Asians and Africans, not because of, but in spite of, the busybody and self-interested interventions of the CRE.

It is not helpful however to be Pollyanna-ish about the race relations prospect. Things will not go so well if significant numbers of the minority communities mimic the angry and irreconcilable attitudes of some of black America. The worst scenario is for them to treat doing well in school as "acting white" and to regard it as "macho" for males to be ruthlessly rapacious and anti-authority.

Fortunately more positive attitudes seem to be winning the day among the ethnic minorities, to judge by comments from some of their leading figures. One thinks of the splendid black athlete Denise Lewis wrapping herself in the Union flag after winning the Olympic gold medal in the women's heptathlon at the Sydney Games in September 2000.

Or of Lord Alli, managing director of Carlton Productions: "I am British, I love my country. I love the Queen. I respect the police. To some, these are controversial statements, but they should not be. There should be no contradiction between being black and being British."

Or of Lord Paul: "I think most of the British people are anti-racism. That is something we should be very proud of. ...I am very proud of being British". (*Daily Telegraph* 10.12.2000.)

Conclusion

Harmonious race relations will not be successfully promoted on the basis of the present regime, which is merely a chapter in the wider imposition of political correctness, is counter-productive and tends to undermine our free institutions. It is important to emphasise that what are claimed to be anti-racist policies are, on balance, actually detrimental to race relations. They are also oppressive towards large and growing numbers of our people, especially those in the public services.

The Commission for Racial Equality is an aggressive self-serving quango, with a vested interest in bad race relations which tend to boost its importance as the soi-disant expert on all ethnic affairs. It increasingly flexes its muscles, and regularly engages in what has rightly been called "ambulance-chasing" to initiate court actions on behalf of alleged victims of racist behaviour. The criterion of fairness to minorities it uses and enforces in a whole range of matters is the racial quota based on the egregious fallacy that equality of opportunity is synonymous with equality of result. This is harmful to the economy and a fertile source of injustice to and resentment by members of the host community.

The use of the quota criterion to label whole institutions "racist" strikes at the roots of the legal order of a free society (which is founded on the idea of personal responsibility) and has created the atmosphere of a witch hunt and fear of persecution among many innocent people.

The CRE, far from improving race relations makes them worse. It should therefore be abolished. I originally recommended a return to the informal, less pretentious but more useful mediating functions of the former Race Relations Board, which was designed to defuse racial tensions. I am now persuaded that any such body, which differentiates groups according to racial origin, does more harm than good. For, however benevolent the intention of its creators, it inevitably falls under the control of minority interest groups to the detriment of the very social harmony it is supposed to promote. It also conflicts with the fundamental principle of a free society: that the law must treat all citizens equally.

For the same reason, the £120 million annual funding of local authority race relations activities should be withdrawn. Only thus can the allegedly anti-racist bureaucracy and its activities, so damaging to inter-ethnic harmony, be curbed.

Further, the whole apparatus of affirmative action, including quotas for jobs and other special, that is privileged, treatment for minority groups, both official and unofficial but in practice obligatory, must be removed, together with official sponsorship of race awareness courses, which do the opposite of what is desirable, which is to promote race unawareness and colour blindness.

Where the EU attempts to impose so-called anti-racist legislation, it should not be incorporated in British law, which, it should be asserted forthrightly, takes precedence over European law in matters of national importance - just as the German judges at their supreme court in Karlsruhe have already asserted the supremacy of German law when it conflicts with European law. The German Court could say this: Germany has not passed section 2 (2) of the European Communities Act 1972. The latter would have to be repealed or amended, or other suitable legislative action taken if and when the new European constitution is introduced.

Immigration matters should be managed in such a way as to serve British interests. The aim should be to accept immigrants, without regard to race or colour, who will make good British citizens and who will make a useful contribution to the economy. This objective will be more difficult to attain while we keep the present arrangements, with the CRE apparat and the divisive, self-defeating, so-called "anti-racist" policies associated with it.

For as long as we retain these policies we shall fail to reap the undoubted benefits which an enlightened immigration policy can bring.

The race relations lobby has demanded, that the government declare Britain to be a multicultural society, that is a society in which all cultures are of equal status. On the contrary it would be more appropriate to declare that Britain, though multi-ethnic and though treating other cultures with appropriate respect and tolerance, is unapologetically a monocultural society in which every citizen of whatever origin is encouraged to participate and contribute to the development of the British way of life.

Present indications are that the so-called "anti-racist" policies will continue to do significant harm both to race relations and to the economy for many years to come. However, in the long run, there is reason to hope that their folly will be recognised and they will either be officially abandoned or fall into disuse. Meanwhile, for a future of happier race relations, we must pin our hopes, not on the meddling of politicians, but on the British people's traditional tolerance, good nature and common sense.

2

A Phobia for Our Time

Every age has its 'isms' and in ours 'racism' has come to the fore. It is an ugly word for what those most given to using it claim to be an ugly feature of Britain today, namely, an unreasoning dislike among the majority white population of ethnic minority groups, especially those with dark skins. That is what it means when used in good faith. Unhappily it is often used not to analyse but to bully, not as an ordinary adjective but as a term of abuse. The point has been well put by Ray Honeyford, former headmaster of Drummond Middle School, Bradford:

> A 'racist' is to the race relations lobby what 'Protestant' was to the inquisitors of the Counter-Reformation, or witches to the seventeenth-century burghers of Salem. It is the totem of the new doctrine of anti-racism. Its definition varies according to the purpose it is meant to achieve. It is a gift to the zealot, since he can apply it to anyone who disagrees with him — and he often ejaculates the word as though it were a synonym for 'rapist' or 'fascist'. It takes its force not from its power to describe but from its power to coerce and intimidate. It is attached to anyone who challenges the arguments or rhetoric of the race relations lobby. It is more a weapon than a word.[1]

Racism is a serious social disease but the recommended cure, anti-racism, can be as fatal. Of course no decent person disputes that racial hatred and strife are deplorable and no one who has any memory or knowledge of the Nazi era can doubt that they have been among the most awful curses ever to afflict mankind. Yet, in this country at least, there is as much reason to worry about the antics of many of those who proclaim themselves 'anti-racists' as about the 'racism' they claim to see all around them. A favourite accusation of those who campaign against racial prejudice in Britain is that this country is one in which racism is firmly institutionalized, indeed endemic in the whole way of life of the majority of its citizens. Yet as much to be deplored is institutionalized anti-racism, the quango kingdom which we have produced to counter what is a very real social problem, but one which through normal human contact should gradually fade.

By 'anti-racism' I mean the doctrine of resistance to the supposed prejudice of the white majority in Britain against its non-white fellow-citizens. This prejudice, it is alleged, produces such oppressive discrimination that violent racial conflict is inevitable unless we as a society accept an interventionist political and administrative regime fundamentally hostile to our traditional free institutions.

A striking statement of this view, remarkable not so much for its extremism, though that is execrable enough, but for its appalling frankness, has been made by Professor Chris Mullard:

> The battle will be a bloody one. Black and white will have no choice. The liberals. . . will be caught in the middle. In the end they too will have no choice — they will have to side with black or white...

> Blacks will fight with pressure, leaflets, campaigns, demonstrations, fists and scorching resentment, which, when peaceful means fail, will explode into street-fighting, urban guerrilla warfare, looting, burning and rioting. Critics will argue smugly that this cannot possibly happen here. Most of them will be white, blind to what is already happening, wrapped in cocoons of isolation and utopian dreams of multi-racialism, confident that white is might.

> To these I say 'Watch out Whitey, nigger goin' to get you!'[2]

The British educationist who wrote these words cannot be

dismissed as an unrepresentative rabble-rouser. On the contrary he was a leading light in the 'anti-racist' movement in Britain. He was Director of the Race Relations Policy and Practice Unit at the London University of Education, Britain's largest teacher-training college, and has since been Professor of Race and Ethnic Relations at the University of Amsterdam.

One object of this book is to expose and to rebut this altogether too prevalent libel of a people unusual if anything for their tolerance and celebrated for their tradition of justice and fair play. Even in the heyday of racialist theories among intellectuals a century ago the British paid hardly any attention to such bogus biology. In Britain no racialist party has ever caught on. In parliamentary elections Fascist and other extreme nationalist parties have never collected more than derisory numbers of votes. All the major parties have shunned racist extremism. There has always been a good deal of *patriotism*, that is love of one's country, among the British, and there still is, though it tends to come to the surface only in times of national danger and surprises even themselves by its intensity, as for instance during the Falklands campaign. Yet in spite of having had for a time an enormous empire, they have precious little missionary urge to impose on others the British way of life.

At its best, British colonialism was distinguished by a policy of indirect rule and live-and-let-live, as far as possible leaving its subjects to abide by their own customs. The exclusiveness of the British colonists' clubs was the reverse side of this coin. And arguably, such exclusiveness was more snobbish than racist: the British middle and upper classes, especially in the Edwardian period, which was also the high noon of empire, were just as exclusive towards the working class at home.

For the sole example of the expulsion from Britain of a

group of people on account of their race one must go back to the thirteenth century when Edward I expelled the Jews. They were readmitted under Cromwell and by the nineteenth century one of their number, Disraeli, had become Prime Minister, and a Tory one at that. During most of their history the British have provided a refuge for those of all races who fled from persecution overseas, including Karl Marx and the proponents of international communism who came to study revolution in the reading room of the British Museum under Marx's watchful eye.

Of course, no one who knows anything about Anglo-Irish history will say that Britain has an untarnished record for racial harmony. But the national flag, the Union Jack, does symbolize the unity in diversity of the English, Welsh, Scots and Irish. Their population movements were certainly not accomplished without conflicts, but in time these have been largely resolved with minimal legislative intervention. Those who moved from one corner of these islands to another made their own arrangements through the free market about food, shelter, leisure and work. And, on the whole, they were gradually assimilated into the surrounding population. By contrast the settlement of the 2.5 million or so immigrants from the New Commonwealth and Pakistan in the interventionist era since the end of the Second World War has created an important new area of state activity and inevitably pushed it into the political domain. A significant fact about Professor Mullard is that so much of his work has been funded by the public purse.

Of course there are many others, mostly less prominent than he and far less objectionable, who are also concerned with race relations and likewise dependent, directly or indirectly, on the taxpayer. These have been collectively dubbed the 'race relations industry', which, not surprisingly, is resented as a cheap gibe by those who belong to or are associated with it. So let it be clear that the object of this work is not to ridicule the efforts of those who sincerely seek better relations between the races but to examine critically and question the highly politicized methods of pursuing that worthy objective in Britain today.

What is or who are the race relations industry? Tom Hastie provides a striking definition:

> By 'race industry' I mean community relations personnel, multi-ethnic education inspectors and advisers, vote-hungry local politicians, members of local government committees and agencies set up for example to monitor police attitudes to blacks, ambitious leaders of immigrant pressure groups and the like. In other words, those with a vested interest in putting race into the forefront of people's minds.[3]

He adds that the result is 'Newsam's Law'[4], which runs, 'The incidence of alleged racism in a given society will vary in a direct proportion to the number of people handsomely paid to find it.' Or, as the old saying bluntly puts it, 'Never ask the barber if you need a haircut.'

It may be objected that this is a case of generalizing on the basis of a few particulars, yet, judging by some of the absurdities which anti-racist extremists have imposed in recent times on the council staff and citizens of boroughs where they have assumed control, Tom Hastie's definition is a fair one. The councils concerned are those with substantial (15% or more) ethnic minorities, and it must be said that, on the whole, the larger the ratio of sectional interests the more radical the council's behaviour becomes. This suggests that they are not so much 'loony left' as is often suggested, but motivated by a perfectly rational desire to win votes. Appeals to a variety of sectional interests — blacks, Asians, gays and Irish supporters of Sinn Fein — are a fairly new phenomenon in part pioneered by Ken Livingstone, leader in the last years of the Greater London Council. He was quite open about his intention of using ratepayers' money to subsidize a constituency of activist minority supporters which added together, especially in local elections where there is normally a very small percentage turnout, could make all the difference between victory and defeat.

The anti-racism mania has become widespread in Britain. To dub it a mania is not unfair. The tone of those in the grip of it is akin to that of the hell-fire preacher: self-righteous and intolerant. Many of them intimidate more than they persuade, and how could it be otherwise? How could anyone expect a teacher to react to a 'race-awareness course' with anything but anger at such an insult to his or her intelligence?

Many of the key figures in the race relations industry are politically motivated, but others have a purely professional interest in magnifying the importance of the task which, after all, keeps them gainfully employed. That would not matter so much were it not for the mounting threat which such people pose to the freedom of ordinary citizens to work or enjoy themselves without gratuitous and, arbitrary interference.

It is no good adopting an attitude of 'let sleeping dogs lie' and assuming that, given time, the problem will simply recede. The race relations industry has a momentum of its own. Those within it who do genuinely believe in the gospel they preach have every incentive to show proof that race relations are getting worse, for that makes their message all the more urgent. Others are not concerned with highlighting racial problems in order that they may be more quickly solved, but are actually in the business of promoting social strife. Instead of integrating the different races into our community these people are seeking to set them against each other. They don't want the foundations of society strengthened but to have them undermined. Their aim is revolutionary and they are thus intent on creating a constituency of malcontents in preparation for the grand assault on our social order which they believe is only a matter of time. This book aims to make their task more difficult and to bring some corrective reasoning into an area where irrational sloganizing has become endemic. In particular I shall try to:

Present the facts which I believe repudiate the charge so often levelled by the race relations lobby that Britain is a profoundly racist society.

Indicate the influence of the race relations industry in Britain, both in its scale and effect.

Show that all too often the activities of the race relations lobby do not advance the interests of the ethnic minorities they are meant to serve, but weaken instead of strengthening their economic position and can even foster popular resentment against the ethnics instead of enlisting goodwill.

Highlight the positive side to the picture, especially the ethnic minorities' successful responses to the demands and pressures of life in Britain.

Argue that the way forward for the immigrant groups is to concentrate on improving their own and their families' material conditions rather than seeking through political activism compensatory privileges and rights.

Suggest an institutional framework for better race relations, including the shrinkage of the Commission for Racial Equality and other lesser bodies and the opening-up of the free market, the great virtue of which is that it is colour-blind.

3

The Roots of Anti-Racism

> Of all the great issues which perplex and divide our society, nuclear weapons, civil liberties and so on, none, I believe, is more dangerous than racism. What makes racism unlike all other political problems is that it is the product of the irrational and is therefore not easily dealt with by ordinary discourse. We are all victims of the poison of racial prejudice. Racism is part of the fabric of our history, woven into our imperial past and although we have shed our colonies — or most of them — we have not succeeded in shedding the ideologies and attitudes which underpinned our economic and military subjugation of other races and cultures. . . We have to recognize — whether we like it or not — that Britain is a multi-racial society.

The above comment is by Jacob Ecclestone, then Deputy General Secretary of the National Union of Journalists, in the foreword of a book produced by the Campaign Against Racism in the Media, with the unlikely and unlovely title *It ain't Half Racist, Mum.*[1] It is characteristic of the approach of many of the anti-racist lobby. It is exaggeratedly alarmist (is racism really the most dangerous issue of our time?). It affects the voice of sweet reason, and by implication contrasts it with the dark irrational urges which are supposed to direct the thoughts and actions of all who disagree with its sentiments. It justifies these sentiments by an appeal to history which is one-sided and little less than a libel on our nation's past. And it ends with an implied threat that, if we know what's good for us, we had better accept the blindingly obvious – that Britain is now a multi-racial society. What, one wonders, does Mr Ecciestone think we were before? To suggest that British multi-racialism is a new phenomenon is, for instance, insulting to the Welsh, an ethnic minority to which this author belongs. It is equally a slight upon the Scots, Irish, Jews, Poles, Ukrainians and numerous others. The whole point about Britain's evolution is that we are publicly and politically one nation but privately a mosaic of coexisting peoples. A British Sikh, Hindu, Muslim, Bengali, Tamil or Barbadian is as welcome as a British Jew, Pole or Irishman. All who accept our public traditions are guaranteed the safety of their private traditions in their own homes, because their home is their castle.

There is no worse advice one can give to any immigrant group in any country than to attack that country's traditions and identity. If I were to emigrate to Australia I would not be a 'wingeing Pom' but a 'fair dinkum Aussie Pom'. If I took off to America I wouldn't expect my offspring to be taught to honour George III. If I went to India, I would treat every sacred cow with proper respect. Most immigrants understand this, especially those who are businessmen and need to cultivate customers — like the Muslim grocer who runs an off-licence. Yet such commonsense is apparently resented by many race relations professionals who feel compelled endlessly to emphasize the separateness of people.

The basic objection to the sort of view propagated by Mr Ecclestone and others is a comparative one. It is in fact easier to be a member of even a visible ethnic minority in Britain than in most countries in the world. I would rather be a Tamil in the United Kingdom than in Sri Lanka, a Sikh in Southall than in New Delhi, a black man in Cardiff than in Kosice, Slovakia (where the gypsies are black to the white Slovak population), or in North India, a Chinese in London than in Malaysia.

Nor should Britain feel any need to apologize for its strong sense of identity, which is neither racist nor ideological. In many countries of the Third World there is much talk about 'nation-building', that is to say the creation of the sort of national unity we have constructed over the centuries. Why then should we be expected to dismantle or deny our nationhood? In a world of nation states, if nationality depends on ideology (as in the former Soviet Union) it becomes oppressive. If it depends directly (as in Nazi Germany) on race, it is also oppressive. Yet if there is no sense of being a nation at all the whole of society falls apart through incoherence or corruption, and often a dictator emerges intent on making nationality respected by force. Our social order is all the better for being spontaneously created. It is an *evolved organic unity* rooted in place, history, tradition, myth and language. We are not Jacobins or permanent revolutionaries determined to remove or destroy what the past has bequeathed to us. We respect the local, the private, the voluntary, that is to say the intermediate institution. We are not obsessed with individual origins or ancestry.

Yet such rational objections to the accusations of the anti-racist lobby leave its members unmoved, partly because many of them are driven by a force which is as irrational as real racism. Extreme anti racists are indeed mirror images of those they are in such a hurry to condemn. They have a similar, missionary urge to cleanse the world of the evil they everywhere profess to see, a similar intolerance and a similar emotional intensity. The question on which this chapter seeks to throw light is why such virulence? For, though there are those of the extreme left who jump on the anti racist bandwagon because they are looking for a political constituency and a source of recruitment for their cause, most are vehemently sincere.

The vehemence of the anti-racist lobby and the genuine response it arouses from the public derive from three potent, even traumatic experiences in our nation's past and the way we have interpreted or misinterpreted them. They are, first, the horrors perpetrated in the name of a truly racist ideology by our Nazi enemy during the Second World War, above all the holocaust, that is, the murder of six million Jews. For years, to identify someone as racist was to associate them with the unspeakable cruelties of Hitler's SS. Second, our history as the creator and then disbander of a colonial empire has influenced people in two ways. For those who took pride either in the powerful empire which made us a world power or in the Commonwealth (which in some eyes gave us the moral leadership of the world), the word racist was an insult to our nation's claim to impartial government. On the other hand, those who regarded Britain's colonialism as a long tale of slavery, oppression and exploitation for which we must now make amends, associated the word 'racist' with 'reactionary'. It identified the person so described as one who wished to return to what the left at least considered the most disgraceful episode in our national history. The former 'patriotic' detestation of racism was most influential in the period immediately after the Second World War, while the latter 'anti-British', and normally left-wing, influence prevailed among anti-racists in more recent times.

The third factor, which has facilitated the growth of anti-racism in Britain, was post-war immigration. This caused many ordinary people who were directly affected to give expression to their dismay, which in turn prompted those whose views had already been formed by their interpretation of the other two experiences vehemently to condemn such utterances.

Turning first to Nazism, this evil creed was from the first overtly racist. Its rationale was a bogus theory of the Germans being a superior Aryan race, a *herrenvolk* destined to lord it over the other peoples of the earth, whom they were to conquer and rule. According to this theory the Jews were a sub-human species, responsible for all the ills of German society, who had above all brought about Germany's defeat in the Great War by stabbing her in the back. Such nonsense was pure scapegoatism and scientifically and historically a contemptible myth. There was no biological basis for the idea of a pure Aryan race; the Germans, like all the other peoples of Europe, had a hopelessly mixed mongrel origin and Hitler himself was hardly an example of the blond superman. In any case the Aryan idea was based not on biology but on linguistics. Far from being the enemies of the Fatherland the German Jews, who were a small minority, were particularly well integrated into German society. They were proud to serve in the Kaiser's army and those who emigrated to America continued to associate with other members of the German community over there, in marked contrast with the Jews from other parts of mainland Europe such as Poland and Russia who, once they arrived in the USA, generally had no more to do with other members of the host nation they had left.

The German Jews' patriotism did not however save them from persecution when the Nazis came to power. Those who were not put into concentration camps fled abroad. Many came to Britain, where it must be said, mainly as a result of a much-resented previous immigration of Jews from eastern Europe fleeing the pogroms of Tsarist Russia and Poland before the Great War, there was a good deal of anti-Semitism. It was found in mild form in a number of popular writers of the time like G.K. Chesterton, Hilaire Belloc and even John Buchan. Nevertheless efforts were made on their behalf. As early as 1933, a fund was opened to place academic refugees in British universities. City bankers were moved to anger by the imprisonment of a Rothschild in Vienna. When the world-famous psychiatrist, Sigmund Freud, arrived in Britain red tape was pushed aside to make him a British citizen and the membership register of the Royal Society, which had never left the society's premises before, was taken to Freud's house for signature. As the historian A.J.P. Taylor put it, 'Nazi treatment of the Jews did more than anything else to turn English moral feeling against Germany.'[2] In the Cambridge Union, the students' debating society, it became a convention that one never told jokes about the Jews, reflecting the feeling that there was nothing funny about people who were being persecuted because of their race. (On one occasion this convention was sorely tried. There was a debate on the situation in Palestine, then part of the British Empire, where the British authorities were being supported against Arab extremists by a Jewish battalion. The Zionist speaker waxed lyrical about the unit's fighting spirit indicated by its motto, 'Charge, charge and charge again'. The members held their breath until relief came when a wit on the other side of the house asked on a point of information whether the speaker wasn't mistaken and the actual motto 'No advance without security'.)

It is a matter of record that the British then and later showed themselves less race-prejudiced than many other nations. They continued to welcome Jewish (and other) refugees during the war, save for a brief period just after the fall of France. This was in marked contrast to the governments of the USA and of the Commonwealth countries, Australia, New Zealand, Canada and especially South Africa, which were particularly restrictive towards Jews.[3]

It is worth noting, incidentally, that the wartime British showed no animosity towards coloured servicemen either, for there is no tradition of hostility against coloured people anywhere in Britain as there is for instance in the southern states of America. Tom Hastie tells a story of how he and a fellow sergeant were stopped in a street in Tunis in 1943 by three black GIs who asked them to be the first to drink from a bottle of brandy they had just bought because they wanted, through them, to thank the British people who had been so good to them. 'They treated us real nice, just like we was their own folks,' said their spokesman.[4]

Those who were old enough at the time to appreciate it will remember the mind-numbing quality of the news of what our soldiers found at Belsen and the further appalling revelations about the systematic murder of millions there and at other camps like Auschwitz and Dachau. We knew that the Nazis were evil but nothing had prepared us for evil on quite this scale. The Nuremberg trials and the capture of a mass of Nazi state documents not only spelt out in horrifying detail how Hitler's minions had carried out these barbaric crimes. They also showed that two million Russian prisoners of war died during captivity and that the Germans had seven and a half million slave labourers from the occupied lands. Furthermore it appeared that this was only the start and that the Nazis had plans for the murder or sterilization of millions more Slavs in order to make room for colonies of the German 'master race'.[5]

There is no truth in the argument that these excesses were due to Germany's being engaged in a life-or-death struggle, for they actually drained resources from the war effort. Had the Germans decided to treat the people in the conquered lands of the East like human beings instead of biological inferiors they might well have succeeded in conquering Russia: when they first arrived in parts of the Ukraine they were welcomed as liberators. The main difference the war made was that it rendered mass slaughter logistically feasible through the acquisition of vast depopulated territories in the East where the process of extermination could be carried out. But there is strong evidence that the Nazis had been planning genocide for the Jews as early as 1927.[6]

It is understandable that faced with this appalling record, many should conclude that racism is the most evil of all types of fanaticism. The left especially has been drawn to this view, and sadly some have sought to monopolize the moral indignation generally felt over the holocaust and to use it for their own ends. Thus, for instance, an ILEA teaching pack on Auschwitz contains a discussion of Neo-Nazis in the modern world in which, as Caroline Cox has pointed out, there are clear implications that the British action in the Falklands War is to be condemned as unequivocally as the murderous activities of the Nazis.[7] There is assuredly a certain readiness on the left to identify their opponents, such as the Conservatives and upholders of the capitalist system, with the Nazis or fascists. This absurd distortion is due to the fact that their view of the matter is highly selective. They overlook or prefer to forget that 'Nazi' was another word for 'National Socialist' and that the instrument for carrying out genocide was the big, powerful interfering state. They also forget that the Nazis have not been monopolists in genocide.

For refutation of the idea that as mass despatchers of humankind the Nazis were unique we have only to turn to the Soviet Union, which was engaged in eliminating the so-called Kulaks, that is farmers opposed to collectivization, and in the great Communist party purges, when the Nazis' scheme was only at the planning stage. It was also on a larger scale: to revise the Old Testament dictum, Hitler killed his millions and Stalin his tens of millions. Again, in the course of his 'land reform' in the early 1950s, China's Mao Tse Tung may have executed as many as fifteen million 'counter-revolutionaries'.[8] In relation to population the worst record of all is held by the Khmer Rouge, the Communist regime in Cambodia led by Pol Pot, who without warning drove the town-dwellers into the countryside, so rightly dubbed the killing fields, in the midst of a blazing summer. As a result about a third of them died.[9]

It now appears that the Western aid which went to help the starving in Ethiopia as a result of the generous campaign by Bob Geldof and others, though it did stop many thousands dying from famine, was also used for 'rural resettlement' — in other words forced collectivization, and removal from one part of the country to another. In the process, according to the French charity Médecins Sans Frontières one fifth of the half-million people exposed to this treatment died.[10]

Most of these operations were carried out not in the name of race but of socialism. There are, however, examples of racial persecution by Communist regimes. Stalin uprooted the Tartars from their Crimean homeland and re-settled them in other parts of the USSR, allegedly as a punishment for collaborating with the German invaders during the war.[11]

The oppression of the people of South Vietnam by the victorious Communist Hanoi regime led, as is well known, to the flight of the boat people, most of them in leaky vessels unfit for the high seas, many of which foundered. What is less widely realized is that, of the million or so who thus risked their lives to get away, seventy per cent were ethnically Chinese.[12]

Many will feel that it is unfair by implication to associate Britain's socialists with the Khmer Rouge. But it is equally unfair to lump ordinary British patriots and anti-anti-racists with the Nazis. Indeed there were links between the Khmer Rouge and the far left in Britain, whereas Britain's patriots were for a time the only opponents of Nazi Germany. Those who are now so vocally 'anti-Nazi' are the political descendants of those who supported the Molotov/Ribbentrop pact and called our finest hour 'an Imperialist war'.

The second influence which provides the emotional fuel of anti-racism is an attitude of guilt towards Britain's imperial past. It is summed up in the word 'colonialist' to describe what is alleged to have been an exploitative relationship with the subject countries. Much is made of the earlier period when slaves were shipped across the Atlantic in inhuman conditions. Yet this is an unbalanced indictment which ignores the fact that British idealists, like Granville Sharpe and William Wilberforce, ran a successful campaign against slavery. This led first to the famous test case of 1772 in which Lord Mansfield declared slavery to be incompatible with English common law. As a result 15,000 negroes living in England were set free and subsequently assimilated into the native British population. The slave trade was abolished in 1807, and slavery in British overseas possessions abolished in 1833, at no small cost to the British taxpayer who footed the bill for compensating slave-owners for the loss of their property.

It is none the less often suggested that we should compensate the present descendants of slaves for the injustices suffered by their ancestors. Yet as Thomas Sowell has pointed out, in the case of American blacks, if the principle of compensation is to make up for the difference in the standard of living due to being transferred from Africa to the USA, 'the grotesque conclusion of this arithmetic might be that the blacks pay whites compensation'.[13]

More often it is argued that Britain and other ex-colonial powers have extracted the wealth of the colonies and should now pay it back in the form of financial and technical aid or raising the value of exports through price-support schemes for primary products. This theory of imperialism is, however, based on the fallacious notion that all forms of trade are a zero-sum game, that is to say no trading partner can gain except at the expense of another. In fact most trade is mutually beneficial and, as Adam Smith pointed out long ago, when allied to a free economic order in which people specialize in the economic activities they are best at, creates the wealth of nations. That is why the

Third World countries which have had the greatest amount of economic contact with the West in the past are now the most prosperous. Singapore and Malaysia, when discovered by the West, were largely uninhabited jungle and swamp interspersed with a few fishing villages. British enterprise, including the introduction of the rubber plant, created the foundations of their present flourishing economies. At the other end of the scale countries like Ethiopia, which have had little connection with the West (except for five years of colonial rule under Mussolini), have remained wretchedly poor. Again, the belief that the colonial powers grew rich simply by plundering the colonies assorts oddly with the fact that two of the richest countries in Europe, Sweden and Switzerland, have never had colonies at all.[14]

In truth the worst legacy of British colonialism is that of its last phase, the period of the imperial government's war — and post-war socialism. Prior to that British rule in the colonies had been for the most part light, economical and *laissez-faire.* It was reluctant to interfere with the customs of the subject peoples and left the native chieftains as far as possible to enjoy their traditional authority. With the Second World War, export licensing was introduced and other controls followed in their wake. Export monopolies and marketing boards were established for major export crops and, though ostensibly intended to stabilize violent price fluctuations, became the means of exacting heavy taxes. The proceeds were spent on more education and welfare, but these funds laid the basis of post-independence totalitarian states, like Ghana. The *dirigiste* breed of civil servants who were in control during the imperial sunset encouraged the advance not of the traditional and tribal leaders, but of the urbanized, articulate, professional politicians who were to take control with the coming of independence. Many of these leaders had little capacity for government and under them their countries grew poorer.

What they mostly did have was the gift of the gab, and in the United Nations they found a ready forum for expounding the thesis, formulated not only by Marxist intellectuals but by a whole body of Western development economists, that the impoverishment of their own countries was due to the depredations of their former colonial masters or, in more updated versions, to the subtler imperialism of Western banks and multinational firms.

The cures advocated for the economic bankruptcy which many of these countries have brought upon themselves are various forms of continuing Western aid. Yet such aid, which goes to governments, and its redistribution effect, as Lord Bauer has classically remarked, are tantamount to taking money from the poor in Western countries to give to the rich in the Third World. Besides, what was not simply pocketed by corrupt politicians and officials was often used to bolster manifestly harmful socialist policies, such as farm collectivization (like that in Tanzania and, even worse, in Ethiopia), and otherwise undermine the incentives to economic advance.

The third propellant behind the rapid growth of anti-racism has been post-war immigration, mainly from the West Indies and the Indian sub-continent, which has brought the coloured minority to five per cent of the total population. Broadly, the response of the native British to the new arrivals has varied according to their number. While the numbers were low the resentment was muted. When the numbers rose and threatened to go higher still there was resentment by many immediately affected and vague unease among the rest. There was rather less animus against post-war immigrants, as far as one can judge from historians' accounts, than against the Irish who came across St George's Channel during and after Ireland's potato famine last century. The crucial factor then as much as in recent times was numbers. At the height of the famine, three hundred thousand Irish passed in one year through the port of Liverpool alone. The native Britons looked at them askance. One source of prejudice was their Catholicism. They were also shunned, quite reasonably in fact, as bringers of disease and, though it is a myth that they built the railways (they were never more than a third of the labour force involved), they were cordially detested by the Scottish and English navvies with whom they competed for jobs and with whom they often had pitched battles. The Stockport riots of 1852, which began when an English mob attacked an Irish-Catholic procession, were among the worst civil disturbances of the nineteenth century.[15]

Let us look at the numbers of immigrants entering the country in the post-war years. In the period 1946-51 460,000 foreigners came to Britain. The largest group, 115,000, was Polish, men who had served alongside our forces during the war and who did not want to return to a homeland under Stalin's heel, despite the Labour prime minister's appeal to them to do so. The Communists, who then had some MPs at Westminster, were very keen to repatriate them, feeling no doubt that it was perverse of them to turn down the opportunity of living in an egalitarian society. In the event they were retrained under a resettlement scheme and, with the help of a labour shortage, swiftly absorbed into the rest of the population.

Some prisoners of war, Germans, Italians and Ukrainians, were also allowed to settle in Britain. Additionally some European voluntary workers were recruited, mostly from refugee camps in Germany, to work here, though under rather stringent conditions. Although there was a high demand for their labour during the post-war boom there was great hostility to these newcomers on the shop floor. There were also several thousand soldiers and seamen from the West Indies and India who had served in Britain during the war, who decided to stay and work and who were generally made welcome. However, such immigration began only slowly, starting with the arrival of the *Empire Windrush* ship at Tilbury in 1948 with 492 immigrants from Jamaica.

The numbers coming in from the West Indies gradually rose to reach an annual rate of 30,000 in 1955 and 1956. They jumped to 98,000 between the beginning of 1961 and the middle of 1962 when there was a rush to beat the Commonwealth Immigrants Act which then came into force, although by then the Asians from the Indian sub-continent were becoming more numerous and the exodus from the West Indies was petering out. Between 1955 and 1968 the total net immigration from the West Indies was 669,640. From then until 1977 318,521 settled here, but as a result of increasing restrictions about four-fifths of those were dependants. By 1984 the total immigration had shrunk and that from the New Commonwealth countries was down to 24,800.[16] (These are of course official figures and do not allow for those who came in illegally.)

The response to this immigration revealed a startling gap between the politicians and the people. The alarm in the constituencies, especially those, in order of importance, in the South East, the Midlands, the North and the North West, for the most part found little echo in Westminster. A Tory minister for the colonies, Henry Hopkinson, was still proclaiming at the end of 1954 that Commonwealth citizens of any colour could say *Civis Romanus sum* and come freely to the mother country. The well-to-do progressive Tory M.P. Humphry Berkeley, when asked if he would like to live in a coloured area, used to say that he already had coloured neighbours — he lived next door to the Indian ambassador.

What brought people and politicians closer together was, inevitably, the latter's need of the former's votes. Some, like Paul Foot in his entertaining study *Immigration and*

Race in British Politics,[17] regarded this conjunction as a
shameful surrender to vulgar prejudice and xenophobia.
But was it? A comprehensive survey conducted by the Institute of Race Relations[18] and published in 1969 indicated
that the attitudes of the British public towards race relations were pretty rational. Nearly three quarters of them
were 'tolerant-inclined' and only ten per cent were strongly
prejudiced against coloured people. Regarding jobs and
housing, the majority wanted no discrimination between
white and coloured people and those who did want it were
invariably the ones who were directly threatened themselves. The survey did point to an apparent irrationality of
the majority who thought that the immigrants were taking
more out of the country than they were putting in — irrational because the immigrants' lifespan in Britain included
a higher proportion of time working and therefore contributing to the economy than the British-born. Yet the view
was not completely groundless, for in the short term any
considerable influx, especially if concentrated in one area,
was bound to put a strain on local health, education, police
and other services.

The eventual introduction of restrictions on immigration
was entirely sensible as a means of avoiding social
disruption resulting from the attempt to digest too many
people of alien ways at one time. That they were adopted
despite the opposition of most politicians is nothing to be
ashamed of but should be seen as a vindication of our
democratic system. Yet the conversion of political pooh-
bahs was slow. The empire men in the Tory party, the
Commonwealth enthusiasts in the Labour party and the
radicals on both sides who didn't want to touch anything
remotely connected with racial prejudice, for a long time
avoided any action to stem the rising immigrant tide. When
forced by public pressure to take the first faltering step in
restriction in 1961 it was with great reluctance. In the wake

of restriction came a quango, known first as the Race Relations Board and later the Commission for Racial Equality, to monitor racial prejudice and bring the more obstinate offenders to court. These bodies could almost be called the revenge which establishment politicians took on the voters for making them bring in immigration controls against their will. In the process, as we shall see, they gave authority to people who had every interest in opposing such controls. For, if race frictions were reduced by such limits on the entry of immigrants, the services of the race relations industry would be in less demand.

It was this feeling that Britain's politicians were failing to provide against a major preventable social problem that caused Enoch Powell to make a speech in Birmingham on 20 April 1968 on the subject of race relations which shattered the complacency of the political establishment. He dwelt on the fears of many whites of becoming a minority in their own land. He spoke of how the number of immigrants, instead of diminishing, would grow so fast that it would not be possible to integrate them. (This proposition, incidentally, shows how far removed he was from being racist, for what racist believes in integration?) Under existing policies, he said, it was like watching the nation building its own funeral pyre. To bring in legislation at this juncture, as Parliament proposed, in order to punish discrimination, was to 'risk throwing a match on to gunpowder'. He urged the adoption of a policy of voluntary repatriation before it was too late. He was filled with foreboding and like the Roman seemed to see 'the River Tiber foaming with much blood' — a prophecy that was in some measure to be fulfilled in the later riots in Bristol, Brixton, Tottenham, Handsworth and Toxteth.[19]

The speech was swiftly disowned by his leader, Edward Heath, not because it was against Conservative party policy but because of its tone. Powell was dismissed from the shadow cabinet at the same time. In the country at large however he became for the majority something of a hero. Letters of support poured in by the sack full. London dockers lobbied their Labour MPs on behalf of Powell. An opinion poll showed that 74 per cent of the sample had agreed with the speech and 69 per cent thought Heath wrong to dismiss him.

The Birmingham speech was a milestone because it brought a matter of supreme concern for many ordinary citizens, which most of their representatives had tacitly conspired to ignore, into the mainstream of party politics. Had it not done so, popular frustrations might well have been enlisted in support of uglier activists, members of the National Front and people of that ilk, who dwell on the sleazy sidelines of the political debate. The country remains in Powell's debt for having refused to submit to the race relations lobby and for so forthrightly repudiating its insistent doctrine that racism is institutionalized in the British way of life. As this chapter has sought to show, by ordinary and comparative as opposed to ideal standards, there is nothing shameful in Britain's handling of the great postwar immigration boom except the failure of our politicians to act in time to limit the social damage caused by its becoming too large comfortably to contain. Indeed, by almost any contemporary or historical comparison, our record of absorbing immigrants was a remarkable success.

4

The CRE and Affirmative Action

Without government sponsorship the race relations industry, like many other largely nationalized concerns, would scarcely exist. So, in chronicling its rise, we have to trace the legislative steps in 1965, 1968 and 1976 which established the core of institutions through which it aims to transform British society. Though the purpose of its authors has not wavered, the organizational picture has lost focus through a bewildering change of names. The Race Relations Board, with which the attempt of government to supervise relations between the races began, was later supplemented by the Community Relations Commission. These two bodies were then merged into the Commission for Racial Equality to which, at local level, Community Relations Councils were linked. Before burrowing into these complexities it is worth reflecting on the revolution such laws and institutions entailed.

In Britain's long history of receiving immigrants this was the first time that the authorities had been involved in regulating the way the native population behaved towards them. There was, admittedly, one precedent for UK legislation against racial discrimination in the Government of India Act 1833 which provided that no one should be denied employment in the Indian Civil Service solely because of his race or colour. However, though this was a British statute, its application was to India.[1] In the past Jews, Flemings, French Huguenots, Irish and many other peoples had arrived and settled without any laws being passed to protect them or supervisory body created to watch over them. Indeed there was some legislating discrimination *against* them such as the Test Act, which kept Jews out of

Parliament, though this was not technically racial since it applied to Catholics and Nonconformists as well. But in general the assumption was that the same law applied equally to all. The liberal state was one in which the laws were few and the ideal, in Locke's words, was that they should be known and certain and not subject to arbitrary individual whim. Samuel Johnson expressed the prevailing scepticism of what law and government could achieve in the lines he added to Goldsmith's 'Traveller':

> How small, of all that human hearts endure,
> That part which laws or kings can cause or cure!

That was before today's big state which rests on the conviction that any problem can be solved by the right kind of law. For most people in Britain today have lived most of their lives under governments which have encouraged the belief that for almost every problem there is a political solution. That is why MPs still groan and grow old before their time under the sheer weight of statutes they are obliged to push through the parliamentary mill. To deal with the consequent increase in regulation, the civil servants (at least until Mrs Thatcher arrived in Number 10) have bred and the judges have multiplied. Yet even this growth in control and supervision could not satisfy the legislative urge of Britain's post-war socialist governments. In addition to laws intended to reform they created supplementary institutions to supervise the enforcement of such laws. These bodies were called quangos, an acronym for quasi-autonomous non-governmental organizations. Their growth under post-war Labour governments was something wonderful to behold.

The statutory race relations organizations were classic quangos. Their growth was classic too. Their beginnings were modest, amounting in the first instance to little more than an exercise in gesture politics; but then they proceeded to expand, largely by fostering demand for their services among the pressure groups. There has doubtless been an element of conspiracy, but their expansion is better viewed as the kind of development which is almost inevitable when sectional interests are allowed to establish themselves inside the government machine.

Their emergence in the swinging sixties was symbolic of a moral sea-change in the nation's affairs. The English, even in the days of minimal government, were not loath to regulate sin, including gambling, drunkenness and above all sex. But, in the traditional catalogue of vice, racism was not to be found. On the contrary it was fashionable in the period before the Great War to express patriotic sentiments in terms of race (though only a few took this seriously as a biological theory); there was no question, for instance, of prosecuting Rudyard Kipling when he wrote his 'Recessional' about 'lesser breeds without the law'.

It is significant that in the sixties major moves towards sexual permissiveness and the first statutory penalty laid down for racism should coincide. Racism is by no means peculiar to our era, but it is surely more of an obsession and a source of guilt in our time than at any other in history. This conjunction of diminishing condemnation of sexual misbehaviour or deviance and increased censoriousness and readiness to penalize words or actions based on racial bias was overseen and to an extent fostered by Roy Jenkins, Home Secretary when most of these changes took place.

An ardent admirer, indeed biographer, of H.H. Asquith, Roy Jenkins was less a socialist than a latter-day version, reincarnation almost, of the nineteenth-century Liberal reformer, except that he promoted some very un-Victorian reforms. With the same rather self-righteous zeal which his spiritual forbears brought to measures for the improvement of the masses he swept aside a whole battery of state-imposed restraints on sexual morals. He introduced easier divorce by conniving at private members' bills, legalized abortion and removed penalties for homosexual acts in private between consenting adults and over the live theatre ended the Lord Chamberlain's control. At the same time this rather stuffy and unlikely apostle of sexual liberation blazed the coercive trail to racial harmony, which he defined 'not as a flattening process of assimilation, but as equal opportunity accompanied by cultural diversity, in an atmosphere of mutual tolerance'. Quite why he considered the natural and spontaneous process of assimilation to be by implication more 'flattening' than legislation imposed and enforced by the mighty bureaucratic apparatus of the state is a mystery. His biographer argues that Jenkins was concerned for Britain's image in the world and took a strongly positive view of the contribution that Commonwealth immigrants, like previous waves of immigrants from the Norman Conquest to the refugees of the thirties, could make in overcoming 'our natural island lethargy'.[2] In the Jenkins view of things, immigration was good for Britain and if people resisted it they should be socially engineered into accepting it. It is not surprising that already, even among his colleagues, the impression was growing that his liberalism bore an arrogant taint. 'Despite all his care,' Barbara Castle noted in her diary, 'his instinctive high-handedness will slip out.'[3]

The first statutory step in obligatory integration in 1965, however, owed less to Jenkins than to expediency. Labour, which had won the 1964 general election with a wafer-thin parliamentary majority, was attempting to project an image of purpose in power while pandering to every interest whose opposition might later rob them of office. Happily for them, their Prime Minister was one of the great survivors of all time, who delighted in setting up enquiries and inventing new committees which, as he once remarked, 'takes minutes and wastes years'.

Labour had taken up a holier-than-thou attitude to the immigration controls introduced by the Tories in 1961. Hugh Gaitskell, leader of the Labour party at the time, denounced the Tory proposals as a 'miserable, shabby, shameful bill'. Barbara Castle condemned it for violating the Commonwealth idea of the free flow of traffic and insisted that Labour would 'get rid of control altogether'.⁴ That approach didn't last long however as the reactions came in from the constituencies. After Harold Wilson succeeded Gaitskell as Labour leader, following the former's sudden death, he accepted that there would have to be controls but took refuge in a formula, which in effect was no more than a fudge, for agreeing restraints on immigration with other Commonwealth governments. In fact the controls were not effective enough and there was growing concern in those areas, especially the West Midlands, where the concentration of immigrants was most intense.

The general election result in 1964 was ominous and revealing. In the midst of a Labour victory one result stood out like a sore thumb — the gain of Smethwick by the Tory, Peter Griffiths, at the expense of Labour's Patrick Gordon Walker, who had represented the constituency for nineteen years. There is little doubt that Griffiths won on the immigration issue and had been able to make much of the fact that Gordon Walker had led the Labour party's attack on the Tory immigration control measures in 1961. Wilson became very indignant about this in the House of Commons and castigated Griffiths as a 'parliamentary leper'. It was an exercise in sheer humbug, as shown by the fact that soon afterwards Wilson began implementing the policy of tighter controls for which Griffiths had campaigned. The consultation with the New Commonwealth countries predictably proved a farce, Maurice Foley, whom Wilson had put in charge of immigrants' affairs, reporting to him that a huge increase in immigration levels was expected. Wilson cut back the number of work vouchers issued under the 1962 Act and, as far as dependants were concerned, reduced the qualifying range.

The Labour leader was by temperament less a political prophet than a fixer. He realized how important it was psychologically for Labour to feel superior to their opponents on the issue of race. Having had to bow to public demand for immigration controls, it was necessary to refurbish their moral credentials in some politically less damaging way. For this reason Wilson issued a White Paper promising a law against incitement to race hatred and the prohibition of racial discrimination.

Such a proposal had already been put forward year after year in a private member's bill by a genuine idealist and anti-colonialist campaigner, Fenner Brockway. It must have given many pause for thought that he, like Gordon Walker, had lost his seat at Eton and Slough, near London, in the 1964 election. According to his autobiography[5] this was due partly to lack of enthusiasm for his stand on race in the local Labour party. It didn't help that his most prominent contribution to debates in the House of Commons was on colonial issues which made some of his constituents think that he cared more about the rights of people overseas (increasing numbers of whom were arriving in Slough looking for jobs) than about those who sent him to Westminster. As he says, 'Only on polling day itself did I learn that in one of the biggest wards, no election committee had functioned because the secretary did not like my views on race.' He himself had no doubt that the determining issue was the arrival in Slough of large numbers of Commonwealth immigrants, though there was no question in this instance, as there had been at Smethwick, of the Tory candidate, Sir Anthony Meyer, playing the race card. It would be truer to say that it played itself.

Following, then, the pattern of the Brockway bills the government's Race Relations Bill proposed to make racial discrimination an offence punishable by a maximum fine of £100 if practised in hotels, public houses, restaurants, theatres, cinemas, public transport and any place of public resort maintained by a public authority. It also made incitement to racial hatred illegal and punishable by up to two years' imprisonment or a maximum fine of £1,000. The Public Order Act 1936 (which had been brought in to deal with the rough-house tactics of Mosley's fascists) was to be extended to cover threatening, abusive or insulting words or behaviour which were likely to cause a breach of the peace.

The incitement to racial hatred part of the bill was not controversial. As a matter of fact it was due less to racist propaganda against coloured people than to anti-Semitic speeches at public meetings in the early 1960s. This change in the law was strongly urged by the Board of Deputies of British Jews.

More disputatious was the proposal to make racial discrimination in public places a criminal offence. The Conservatives opposed this, preferring a policy of conciliation. Perhaps because this approach was also supported by the Campaign Against Racial Discrimination and the Labour lawyers, the government modified its bill. In the new draft, in order to secure compliance with the anti-discrimination provisions, the Race Relations Board was conceived, though its actual birth was attended by complications.

It is hard to believe that Harold Wilson saw the Race Relations Act which then passed with opposition support as anything more than a very useful public relations exercise. Honour was satisfied, the lobbies, chattering classes and even the Tories were placated. At the same time the act's limited range of application should mean that it would not upset the all-important average voter, and what resentment did occur could be absorbed by the Race Relations Board, leaving the government unscathed.

Its main merit was as a safety-valve. That was how the Home Secretary, Sir Frank Soskice, who had guided it through its various stages, evidently saw it. Summing up he said: 'We have taken what in a sense is a first step. I hope that events will show that it is not necessary to take any further step and that this may be the last step. If the bill turns out to be a successful Act of Parliament and to achieve its purpose, it will, by a paradox. . . very rarely need to be called into operation.' It would, he reflected, be 'an ugly day in this country' if they had to come back to Parliament to extend the legislation's scope.

Alas for Sir Frank's optimism! That 'ugly day' was to come far sooner than he expected. He reckoned without the growth potential of all bureaucracies whenever they're given the chance. He also, to amend a phrase of Walt Whitman's, overlooked 'the infinite audacity of unelected men', especially the race relations pressure groups, who were already planning to expand the functions of the board far beyond what Sir Frank had envisaged. Another factor was his own ill-health, which meant that he soon resigned and his place as Home Secretary was taken by Roy Jenkins, a great admirer of the Kennedy/Johnson administrations' affirmative action approach to racial affairs, which admittedly was not then so evidently the disaster it later became.

The original idea had been to appoint an obviously independent chairman to the Race Relations Board, partly to counterbalance the other two members, Sir Learie Constantine, the famous former West Indian cricketer, and Dr Joost de Blank, former Archbishop of Cape Town and apartheid campaigner. For both these gentlemen, however eminent, were too much cast in the role of crusaders to be considered wholly impartial. The trouble was that, to start with at least, nobody of stature wanted to take the top job.

It was turned down both by Lord Selkirk and Kenneth Younger. Jenkins solved the problem by appointing an old Oxford friend, Mark Bonham-Carter, a well-connected Liberal (brother-in-law of Jo Grimond, the Liberal leader, and grandson of H.H. Asquith), who had recently lost his seat.

By the time Bonham-Carter took over Dr Joost de Blank had resigned and Mr B.S. Langton, former Mayor of Manchester, had been appointed in his place. He and Sir Learie were only part-timers. Bonham-Carter's salary was only £4,000 a year and the modesty of the establishment was shown by the fact that it did not qualify for a switchboard. The annual bill for salaries, fees and other expenses for the whole organization was only £35,000. The race relations lobbies, however, were determined that it should not stay that way. One of the more ominous developments was that the Campaign Against Racial Discrimination (CARD) was planning to form groups to uncover cases of discrimination and to open a complaints office with white volunteers ready to apply for houses and jobs refused to coloured applicants. This *agent provocateur* activism was far removed from the minimal interference hoped for by Sir Frank Soskice when he summed up the debate on the third reading of the act.

There seems little doubt that Jenkins and Bonham-Carter thenceforth co-operated with the pressure groups to extend the functions and powers of the board. Both the board and the National Committee for Commonwealth Immigrants (set up under the chairmanship of the Archbishop of Canterbury on 1 April 1964) produced reports in 1967 calling for an extension of the anti-discrimination law to other fields, including housing, employment, home loans and insurance. They then jointly financed research by Political and Economic Planning which did a sample survey in six cities and reached similar conclusions. These were further supported by a group of lawyers in the Street Report, also financed by the board and national committee.

It was suspicious that the survey of Race Relations, which contained a careful investigation by Research Services Limited showing, broadly, how tolerant the British people were towards immigrants, had its preliminary results appear only after the second Race Relations Bill was published and only just in time for the Commons debate. For by that time, since the government had decided to back it, the legislation was a *fait accompli*. In the survey a nationwide sample showed that a large majority were against discrimination on grounds of colour in the most vital areas of jobs and housing. Further, colour prejudice in general was found to be lower among the younger than the older age groups, a hopeful sign for the future. This hardly squared with the conclusion of the PEP Report — that there was substantial discrimination against coloured people — one of the two pillars which supported Jenkins' case for having the bill at all.

Although the draft bill had been drawn up at the Home Office under Roy Jenkins, his departure for the Treasury meant that the task of pushing it through the Commons fell to his successor, James Callaghan, who did not have quite the same enthusiasm for its aims. The bill, though it duly got through, had by no means a trouble-free passage. For one thing it had been preceded two months before by something approaching a panic measure to control immigration of East African Asians, large numbers of whom, after independence in Kenya, Uganda and Tanzania, were found to have the right to passports letting them enter Britain, and likely to make use of that right owing to persecution by their governments. Certainly the number of Commonwealth immigrants had risen sharply, from 63,211 in 1965 to 74,977 in 1967 (Home Office statistics). As a result the bill looked like a sop to liberal opinion to compensate for surrendering to popular clamour for further immigration control. Moreover Enoch Powell had made his controversial Birmingham speech three days before the Commons debate.

The act which finally emerged made racial discrimination in housing, employment and services such as insurance and credit facilities illegal. It also banned the 'no coloureds' kind of advertisement and made it illegal for a hotel-keeper to refuse a room on racial grounds. The Race Relations Board was to be enlarged — its existing £60,000 grant was trebled — and there was to be an additional body, the Community Relations Commission, to concentrate on fostering racial harmony and to advise and make recommendations to the Home Secretary on matters affecting community relations. Mark Bonham-Carter, who had earlier complained that the board was not empowered to act on one in five of the complaints that it received, had now obtained the additional role, powers and staff for which he had campaigned.

All the extra bodies were soon required to deal with a veritable torrent of complaints from people claiming to be victims of racial discrimination. Did this show how much the changes were needed? There is little reason to think so. First, there is the elementary point that where there is a demand for a commodity or service, the market will supply it: this applies to complaints of racial discrimination as much as it does to hamburgers. Second, many of the complaints were time-wasting and absurd, which suggests that genuine complaints were in short supply.

One of the incidents early reported to the board concerned a country-inn landlord in Cambridge, a ripe character John Hollick de la Taste Tickell. He was locally known as 'the squire of Whittlesford', a village in Cambridgeshire, and wore eighteenth-century knee breeches behind the bar of his pub, the Tickell Arms. He had a row with a coloured student during Cambridge university's May Week, when a Trinidadian accompanied by a white girl from Homerton training college came in too late to be served lunch. In the altercation that followed, Tickell, according to his own account, said that if the chap didn't like the way England was run he could go back to his own country — 'But this was no more than I would have told a Scotsman or an Australian in similar circumstances.' Tickell continued:

> I am a fervent supporter of Enoch Powell, but this remark certainly had nothing to do with the colour of the student's skin. Why, I've even danced with Princess Elizabeth of Toro [Uganda's first woman barrister] at a party given by Lord Birdwood. And you can't get much blacker than she is, the beautiful girl. Fortunately my public house is most popular with the undergraduates — Indians, Africans, Siamese and Chinese come in here. Some have already offered to give evidence on my behalf.[6]

More notorious was the case of an Eastbourne doctor who put an advertisement in *The Times* personal column for a 'Scottish daily help able to do plain cooking including porridge'. The Race Relations Board ruled that it should have read, 'Daily for Scottish family able to do some plain Scottish cooking'. This fatuous piece of sub-editing was attacked in the House of Commons by the member for Eastbourne, Sir Charles Taylor, who said of the board, 'All these bumptious asses should be removed.' He went on, 'We remember Mr Mark Bonham-Carter, when he sat on the bench behind me, and we realized then that he had little sense of humour.' On reading of the case, Mr Bill Feazey, a butcher in Bexley, Kent, immediately reacted by placing an advertisement in one of his shops for a 'Scottish butcher able to cut Scottish meat', in the hope of being reported to the Race Relations Board so that he could expose how ridiculous it was.[7]

In November 1969 there were complaints about a TV comedy show called 'Curry and Chips' starring Spike Milligan as a Pakistani immigrant, in which there were references to 'coons and wogs'. In this instance, a board official was wary and said he did not think the board should become involved, but it was not the last he was to hear of it.[8] Two months later the issue was raised again by Clive Jenkins, joint General Secretary of the Association of Scientific, Technical and Managerial Staffs. But he was too late: the series had ended on Boxing Day.

Already in the first year of the bill it was becoming apparent how inadequate general rules about racial discrimination often are to deal with the complexities they are designed to regulate. For instance there was the case of a photographer who refused to take coloured clients. The photographer maintained that this was not due to colour prejudice but to the fact that coloured people wanted him to provide extra lighting to make their skins look fairer and at seven shillings and sixpence a time he couldn't afford it.[9] A Pakistani accused of race prejudice because he put a notice reading 'Wanted — English Lodger' in his front window was acquitted when it was found that he wanted an English lodger to teach his five children English.[10]

The board showed its mettle, though, in April 1970 when it moved in swiftly to stop members of Gentleshaw and Cannock Wood Women's Institute in Staffordshire from singing 'Ten Little Nigger Boys' in a talent contest. Nothing daunted the women from the villages near Lichfield substituted 'golliwogs' for 'nigger boys' and won third prize.[11]

The growing number of trivial cases began to worry the board, not as an indication that there might be some basic flaw in the system but because they led to the assumption that no one was taking racial discrimination seriously. And indeed in January 1970 someone played a hoax on firms all over the country, sending them letters with Race Relations Board headed notepaper ordering them gradually to increase their employment of immigrants to twenty-five per cent by 1980, sacking white workers if necessary to achieve this result.[12] Similarly no one was sure whether Wilf Proudfoot, the Tory MP for Brighouse and Spenborough, was being serious or pulling everyone's leg when he complained to the BBC that it provided nineteen hours a week of broadcasting in Welsh compared with only one and a half in Hindi and Urdu, though Britain had far more speakers of the latter two languages than of Welsh. What was the board to do if the English girls at Henley College of Further Education fulfilled their promise of presenting their petition complaining that they were not allowed to wear trousers while the Asians girls were?[13]

Young bachelors could get into trouble too. One such advertised in a Brighton newspaper for 'an attractive girl-friend of European origin'. A complaint was sent to the Race Relations Board by middle-aged Mr Alan Hancock, an engineer of Lower Rock Gardens, Brighton, who claimed that the advertisement contravened the Race Relations Act, but added, 'The effect of my action may be to demonstrate that the act is absurd.'[14]

That was a feeling widely shared. It seemed that the most innocent of transactions could be found to contravene the act and all sorts of simple souls suddenly descended on by race relations officials demanding to know if they realized that they had been breaking the law of the land. In March 1971 Mr Jack Tamburro, an accordionist at the Vineyard Restaurant in Birmingham, advertised for an Italian singer to join a trio. The advertisement said that an English singer would also be considered but there was a complaint that this discriminated against any singer who was not Italian or English. The point was, of course, as a bemused Mr Tamburro made clear, that it didn't really matter what race the person was provided he could sing fluently in Italian.[15]

Why should clanking officialdom ever have got involved in such a minor affair? The old legal motto *De minimis non curat lex* — the law is not concerned with trivia — was something which the race relations industry had never fully grasped. Senior figures at the Race Relations Board continued to be worried about the trivial cases that were arising because they feared that they would bring the law of race relations into disrepute, especially among the immigrant community. What did not seem to have occurred to them was that the absurdity was not the result of mischief but inherent in the race relations law itself. It had been given wide-ranging yet vague jurisdiction over what people had long considered to be an extensive but private realm where only their own personal standards prevailed. If a law is to be effective it must mirror a moral consensus, not impose a standard which the majority rejects. It cannot command respect if it enters a sphere of human activity where most people consider that it has no business to be. A law needs to be precise, so that people know exactly what their obligations are, not blurred, inspirational and brimful of optimism that those over whom it holds sway will have a change of heart or be born again. It was because it did not measure up to such commonsense criteria, because it deserted them for the more alien concepts of law as an auxiliary to a crusade, that the law had become such an ass.

Let us turn for a moment to the Community Relations Commission — the new junior partner for the Race Relations Board created by the 1968 Act. Considering that its task was to foster felicitous relations between the races, the appointment as its first chairman of the abrasive Frank Cousins, retiring boss of Britain's largest union, the TGWU, seems in retrospect decidedly strange. Nowadays, after so many years of Mrs Thatcher, we tend to forget what pooh-bahs those old union barons used to be. His official, painstaking biographer, Geoffrey Goodman, suggests the appointment was due to Cousins being 'of course, profoundly committed to fighting racial prejudice'. The only example he offers of this commitment was to do with the London busmen in Cousins' own union, and the details are sparse.[16] Otherwise it was apparently based on the sentiment generated long ago by an Indian doctor who once restored his injured mother. It seems more likely that his was just a routine quango appointment selected from the Labour government's list of the Great and the Good. It might also have owed something to the fact that the job was in the gift of James Callaghan, who was at the time ingratiating himself with the union chiefs whom he was soon afterwards to gratify by blocking Barbara Castle's 'In Place of Strife' scheme for union reform. In any case Cousins was the wrong man for the job. He upset the staff with his imperious ways. He couldn't see why the CRC should be separate from the board and like a typical TGWU boss wanted a merger.

He had no time for a body which was all propaganda and no muscle, and thought that the operation was hopelessly small and underfunded. Yet the accounts for the year 1970 showed that it had underspent its annual allowance of £350,000 by £22,000.

In 1970 Jeff Crawford, a leading figure in the West Indian Standing Committee, wrote to Cousins tactfully suggesting that he should resign on health grounds and give way to a younger man. By November this is what he had done, with Mark Bonham-Carter moving over from the board to fill his place. A few months later a top mandarin, John Burgh, was drafted in as Deputy Chairman. A still more senior civil servant took Mark Bonham-Carter's vacant chair at the Race Relations Board. This was Sir Geoffrey Wilson, a former Permanent Secretary at the Ministry of Overseas Development, described in *The Times* as a 'bureaucrat's bureaucrat'. With his radical Quaker background and one-time close connection with Labour's most puritanical Chancellor of the Exchequer, Sir Stafford Cripps, he could hardly fail to have acquired a sense of moral superiority which was appropriate to his new job.

The arrival of these high-powered functionaries signalled the beginning of a quieter period in the history of the board and the commission. In its annual report published in July 1971 the board was optimistic that, since the number of complaints received was down from 1,549 to 1,024, the initial surge of racial discrimination complaints had spent itself and that the frivolous ones were at last phasing out. In truth the reduced tempo more probably reflected the change of atmosphere which came with a new government after the Conservatives won the 1970 general election. For the Conservatives, though pledged to further racial harmony, were not especially enamoured of the race quangos (a word not yet in use) and were evidently not going to encourage them in their sillier quests. Indeed, had it not been for the fact that the Race Relations Board had been forced down Edward Heath's throat by the fuss over Enoch Powell, whom he disliked, it might have had a much thinner time.

In the eyes of most people such cases indicated that the staff of the Race Relations Board were wholly unrealistic. And if it was the law that was at fault then what kind of a law was it which gratuitously stirred up trouble between the English, Scots, Irish and Welsh? Yet the board, far from relenting, was now engaged, though not very successfully, in pursuing cases of discrimination in private clubs. The board's annual report also invariably demanded that it should have wider powers. Its paternalist tone was unwavering and was particularly noticeable when it argued in its report published in mid-1982 that most victims did not complain because (like Molière's Monsieur Jourdain who had no idea that he was speaking prose) they did not realize that they were suffering discrimination. It was also apparent that the board felt the government was not doing enough about consulting its race relations bodies, on immigration policy for instance, though on that issue many MPs thought it would do better to consult the electors. The constant theme was the demand for more powers. In this respect the most persuasive case was for the discretionary power not to investigate a complaint where in the board's view no useful purpose could be served. This would have avoided the more fatuous publicity-stunt complaints, yet the corollary was that no citizen could then be denied the right to pursue a racial discrimination suit in the courts. That, however, would work against the spirit of the 1965 Act which was trying to minimize racial conflicts by treating them as a public wrong to be settled as far as possible by conciliation. As Sir Frank Soskice had said in the debate when the 1965 legislation was going through, it would be 'a mistake to open the door to individual complaints which could be pressed further and further'.

Other demands for additional powers looked more like empire-building. Arguing that it was better to stop unlawful discrimination before it happened, the board sought authority similar to that of factory inspectors to investigate an establishment on suspicion that the law was being breached. The Home Secretary during the Heath government, Robert Carr, however, thought the board had quite enough power already. His main concern was to avoid provoking a sharp polarization of public opinion. At that time he was busy damping down fears of repatriation of illegal immigrants (brought about by Enoch Powell's campaign) and had instructed chief constables around the country to go easy on the search for them. While this was going on he had no call for a rejigged Race Relations Board stirring the pot and enraging the Tory right, some of whom already saw it as a haven for black-power agitators.

With the collapse of the Heath administration in 1974, the return of Labour to power and the reinstallation of Roy Jenkins in the Home Office, the board's pleas for an increasingly interventionist policy on race had a more sympathetic hearing. The response, though, was not necessarily to the board's taste. The all-party Select Committee of MPs reporting in June 1975 said that the Race Relations Board and the Community Relations Commission had failed and should be scrapped. Alas, this flash of wisdom was brief: the committee sought to put a new, much larger, Equal Rights Commission in their place. (Curiously enough a high-powered Tory committee had earlier recommended something similar to Edward Heath, except that it wanted to retain the board and make it responsible also for women's rights. One joker commented that the suggestion had taken this form because it would be more appealing to testy old bachelor Heath, who viewed women as members of a different race.)

Roy Jenkins went further than any of his predecessors and created an Equal Opportunities Commission, in addition to reshaping the race quangos. In the latter case he followed the recommendation of Lord Rothschild's Central Policy Review Staff, that the Race Relations Board and the Community Relations Commission should be merged. The objection to such a merger was that it would muddle the two functions for which the two bodies stood, mixing up the 'policeman's' role of the board with the educative and fact-finding task of the commission. The reply of the merger enthusiasts was that this was to mistake the role of the policeman, who should be as much concerned with the prevention of crime by the alleviation of its causes as with law enforcement.

So the merger went through and out of the ashes of the Race Relations Board and the Community Relations Commission, there arose, phoenix-like, the Commission for Racial Equality, the whole of which was larger than the two former parts. This was because it had a more ambitious role. The new act prohibited racial discrimination in employment, training, education, housing, the provision of goods, facilities and services and advertising. And the new body acquired machinery similar to that provided in the Sex Discrimination Act for assuring equal opportunities for women.

Meanwhile the flow of immigrants into the country (which had fallen after the Conservative Immigration Act of 1971 from the previous level of 63,000 a year to 34,044 in 1973) was, as a result of certain relaxations, such as the right of Indian women to bring in their fiancés, again on the rise. Estimated to be running at 50,000 a year, all the signs were that the figure was about to increase dramatically. In a Commons debate on the subject in May 1976 Enoch Powell made the shock revelation of an internal report by a Home Office official, Mr Charles Hawley, who had gone to India to assess the waiting lists of dependants applying for entry to Britain. The Labour Minister of State concerned, Alex Lyon, had estimated in 1975 that the waiting list was 180,000, which could disappear in two years. Hawley, however, reported that new applicants were appearing as fast as entry certificates were granted. It was well known that certificates could easily be bought, and, given the Indian joint family system, arranged marriages, and the loose British definition of 'dependant', there was every justification for Powell's comment in the debate (which provoked cries of 'fascist') that 'far from emptying a finite pool' they were 'trying to bail out the ocean'.[17]

Today's discrimination-phobia is surely related to the

habit of describing all human differences as 'inequalities'. The effect of this is to pass from recognizing that one thing is not the same as another to a more traumatic situation where any difference is assumed to be bad because it offends against the egalitarian ideal.[18] Yet, 'We cannot avoid every sort of distinction or discrimination. If we set out to establish equality in one respect, we shall establish some other inequality in another respect.'[19] The classic illustration of this was in Communist countries, where the economic inequalities of property-ownership were exchanged for far greater political inequalities, with life-or-death powers placed in the hands of the Communist party and the secret police. Similarly, though of course far less spectacularly, the suppression of alleged race-based inequalities has called for the establishment of a new inequality of power between the members of the race relations industry and the rest of society, over which its trustee, the Commission for Racial Equality, has obtained novel discretionary power. For, under the Race Relations Act of 1976, the CRE's remit was not only extended to cover employment, education, the provision of goods, services and property. It was also authorized formally to investigate and to serve any organization merely suspected of discrimination with a non-discrimination notice (though often it was only necessary to threaten to issue one) which could be enforced in the courts. These powers were likened by Lord Denning on one occasion to those of the Spanish Inquisition. People who (like the authors of a Fabian tract[20] on the subject which referred to Denning's comment as 'a flight of fancy') are unmoved by these strictures, might take more notice of the comment of Mr Alex Lyon, the former Labour minister. When he was on the Home Affairs Committee which examined the Commission for Racial Equality in 1981, he said that the CRE had been given the strongest powers of enforcement of law against racial discrimination in the

Western world and went on to ask what it had done with them. We must ask the same question today.

Here is a body which was set up with the duty of increasing racial harmony. It was given substantial resources. Thus in the CRE's first full year, 1978-9, its budget was no less than £4.9 million, rising to £9.4 million in 1985-6. It was required to pursue racial harmony in two main ways. First it was to use its wide-ranging semi-judicial powers, inquisitorial and prosecutorial, though in a conciliatory spirit, to ensure that the law against racial discrimination was obeyed. Second it was to campaign for an end to racial strife and educate the public into dropping its prejudices based on race.

In its first decade of endeavour the Commission for Racial Equality was, to put it mildly, unsuccessful. It could hardly be said to have contributed to racial harmony when the period of its existence saw the worst race riots in our history. As recently as January 1985, CRE chairman Peter Newsam, surveying the twenty years since the first Race Relations Act was passed, said that racism was getting worse. In support of this contention he mentioned the increasing barracking of black footballers, which had spread from London to Scotland, and the minimal coverage of Britain's black Olympic talent. In his annual report twelve months later he said 1985 would be remembered as a year in which there were serious riots in four inner-city areas. He implied, of course, that it was all the fault of the government, but his own organization, set up specifically to improve race relations, had, far from contributing to that end, been a major part of the problem. In countless instances its efforts had been counterproductive, creating resentment out of all proportion to the 'injustice' it imagined itself to be correcting.

The CRE likes to present its work as so many investigations and cases pursued, so many correctives to racial prejudice administered, so many promotional exercises to enlighten a benighted public completed. Yet the psychological effect on both the host community and the ethnic minorities has been disastrous. As Andrew Alexander admirably put it,

> We have thus now reached the stage where the official and not just the unofficial parts of the race relations industry have one overriding aim: to make us all eat, breathe and sleep 'race'. . . For though the race relations industry may not have succeeded in improving race relations — it has made them vastly more prickly and vastly worse — it has succeeded brilliantly in one thing: making people dead scared of the accusation of being 'racially prejudiced'.[21]

Much of the commission's attention is centred on discrimination in employment. A code of practice which it issued to guide employers would, if followed, require them (or some senior member of the firm who, it is recommended, should be appointed to give attention to matters of race) to spend nearly their whole working day puzzling over whether they have been discriminating unknowingly. For instance, failure to tell the doorkeeper to treat job applicants who arrive at the factory all the same way, might get the management into trouble. Advertisements of vacancies should begin with the ritual declaration that the employer is an equal-opportunity employer and declare no preference for any particular sort of employee. The problem is that almost any job specification could be charged with discriminating against some racial minority — in advertising for a tall basketball player, for instance, would one be discriminating against pigmies?

Especially sinister is the covert attempt to oblige employers to accept the idea of racial quotas. Employers are recommended to monitor regularly the ethnic composition of their workforce, not just overall but in 'each plant, department, section, shift and job category and [to monitor] changes in distribution over periods of time'. They are also advised to keep detailed reasons for acceptance and rejection at each stage of the selection process to ensure that no decisions have been influenced by racial factors.

The object of monitoring, it is made clear, is to ensure that ethnics are not 'under-represented', which means not present in the same proportion as they are in the population as a whole (whether district, region, or nation as a whole is not spelt out). Of course there is no earthly reason why the proportion of ethnics in a firm should correspond to that of whatever larger unit of population the lawmakers had in mind. For the qualities demanded of workers are not necessarily distributed evenly throughout society. The guide also gives the impression that monitoring and operating a quota are *expected* of companies; even though no such legal obligation exists. The 'code of conduct' is thus a mixture of deception and intimidation.

Many of the cases the CRE chose to take to court showed an incredible lack of commonsense. For instance, in 1982 the CRE ruled that the word 'Christian' was impermissible and grounds for legal action when a doctor advertised for a partner who should be a Christian. It later transpired that a dentist had earlier been warned on identical grounds. This was not only offensive but itself indirectly racist, for the ludicrous assumption was that if you were Christian you must be white.

Another complaint lodged by Mr Donald McGrath, a member of the Brent Irish Advisory Service, which the CRE took up and sent to the Attorney General on the grounds that it stirred up racial hatred, concerned a publication called *The Official Irish Joke Book Number 3 — Number 2 to follow*. The sorts of jokes which aroused the CRE's concern were as follows:

What do you call an Irishman with half a brain? — Gifted.

> There was the Irishman who tried to gas his wife by throwing her into the North Sea.

> Did you hear about the Irish firing squad? They formed a circle.

Sensibly the Attorney General, Sam Silkin, gave his opinion that though the jokes were insulting to the Irish it would be impossible to launch a prosecution. There was no prospect of success in proving that hatred would be stirred up by the book.[22]

A similar case was brought by a Merseyside teacher, who was also race relations officer for the Liverpool National Union of Teachers, against the publishers of *Roy of the Rovers*, the ageless hero of the schoolboy comic strip. It concerned an incident in one of the stories when Melchester Rovers, on tour in the Middle East, had six of their players killed in a terrorist bomb attack. This story was alleged to stir up racial hatred against the Arabs. The outlook of anyone who could spend time and effort on such a farcical prosecution attempt (he even said that if the act was not strong enough to sustain it, it would have to be revised) certainly takes some fathoming.[23]

More important was a case which went to the Appeal Court in July 1982, concerning the refusal of a Birmingham private school to admit a Sikh boy unless he removed his turban and cut his hair.[24] The CRE alleged that this was racial discrimination, though there was no doubt that the school was multi-racial. The Appeal Court, presided over by Lord Denning, decided that a Sikh was not a member of a racial group for the purposes of the act — a blow for commonsense. There was, it decided, no racial discrimination involved, merely a matter of everyone being subject to the same school rules. If the school had been forced to accept the boy then that would have amounted to favouritism. It would have meant that Sikhs were being given a special dispensation to break a rule which everyone else had to keep. That is what Enoch Powell had earlier called 'Communalism' — the giving of privileges to minority groups which are denied to the majority population. Far from improving race relations that kind of thing harms them by suspending the pressures towards conforming with the *mores* of the host community and thus hindering the process of integration. It was extraordinarily perverse of the CRE, but unfortunately quite consistent with many of its other initiatives, to attempt in this way to put up barriers against assimilation, which is where the main hope for harmonious race relations in the future surely lies.

Many have been appalled by the waste of public money involved in the commission's relentless pursuit of hopeless cases. One such was Lord Diplock giving a judgement against the CRE in June 1982. The CRE had gone to the Lords in an attempt to reverse the judgement of the Appeal Court over alleged racial discrimination in Hillingdon. The council of that borough was at its wits' end because it was statutorily obliged to house the homeless who arrived there and, since London Airport was nearby, it bore the full brunt of the large numbers who were arriving by air from abroad. That was bad enough without having the CRE descend on it with additional complaints about its discriminating against some of the immigrants because of their colour, especially when, as Mr Terence Dicks, the council's housing committee chairman, claimed, the CRE's procedures were like those of the 'Star Chamber'[25].

The high-handedness of many of the CRE's investigations and legal actions was often compounded by the costs which it inflicted on those it had in its sights. In December 1981 Mr Maurice Hulks, chief executive of the Conservative-controlled Slough borough council, wrote to the Minister of State at the Home Office to complain that the commission had abused its powers. A two-year inquiry which it had mounted into Slough's housing policy and abandoned without reaching any conclusion had cost the council £20,000 in legal advice and paperwork. The commission then proposed to institute a second inquiry with slightly different terms of reference but covering much the same ground.[26]

Anger with this sort of behaviour by the CRE found expression in an attempt to introduce a bill for its abolition. It was presented by the Conservative MP Ivor Stanbroke, who described the commission as one of the worst quangos and alleged that it did the opposite of what it was set up to do by emphasizing racial differences and thus promoting discord. He quoted as an example the experience of a London employer who had asked a Job Centre to find him a clerical assistant. There were thirty-two applicants, thirty-one of whom were coloured, and none was found suitable. The CRE then sent the employer thirty-one forms, one for each of the coloured applicants who had not been appointed, demanding to know why not.[27]

Mr Stanbroke's move did not succeed but it was indicative of a widespread and deep-felt irritation with the CRE, which was not only considered incompetent after the 1981 Home Affairs Committee examination of it (which we shall come to shortly), but also to be increasingly authoritarian. This emerged in its bizarre legal contest with the Home Office over its power to investigate immigration procedures.

The CRE had first become concerned with this issue following the widely-publicized 'virginity test' applied to an Indian woman at London Airport in February 1979, as a means of checking whether she had genuinely come to England to marry her fiancé as she had claimed. In fact the Home Office maintained that the purpose of the examination was to determine whether the woman had borne children, not whether she was a virgin. Their assumption was that an Indian woman would not have had children outside marriage; if she was found to have had children she must be married already and could not be a fiancée. As a result of the publicity surrounding the test, the Home Office issued instructions that there were to be no more such examinations and arranged for a full enquiry to be made into the use of medical examinations in immigration control.

The matter should have stopped there, but the CRE saw it as an opportunity to raise the question of racial discrimination in immigration control generally. It called on the Home Secretary to institute a public enquiry. When this was not forthcoming it announced its intention to embark on an investigation itself. The Home Office countered with the assertion that immigration was outside the commission's powers because 'Immigration controls do not affect the equality of opportunity of those established here and are not concerned with the interaction of different racial groups.' The matter went to the High Court where Mr Justice Woolf ruled that the commission might conduct the proposed investigation but pointed out that it was not likely to get very far if co-operation by the Home Office was refused.

The chairman of the CRE had already said that the enquiry would not trespass upon immigration policy. As *The Times* commented, the only reason for the Home Office not to co-operate could be that 'it did not trust the commission's discretion or good intentions'. It added that the Home Office did entertain such doubts 'it must be said frankly that the commission's reputation is not of the highest'.[28] To put the matter a little more bluntly, the commission was obviously making a naked bid for power. It was seeking to wrest control of immigration policy from the politicians and turn it on its head. For whereas all politicians, whatever they had said in opposition, once in power ended up

limiting New Commonwealth immigration on the principle all along espoused by Enoch Powell — that assimilation of immigrants was only possible if the numbers were
controlled — the CRE was consistently putting forward
the diametrically opposite view: that improved race relations would result if immigration policy were more lax.[29]
When its investigation was published in 1985 the key recommendation was: 'There should be a major change of
emphasis in the operation of the procedures, giving less
priority to the prevention of evasion and overriding priority to ensuring that genuine applicants are enabled to exercise their rights with the minimum of delay and difficulty.'
This change of emphasis included 'explicit guidance and
instruction' to immigration officers that 'inconsistencies
in applications arising from efforts to cover up past tax
frauds should not delay the issue of entry clearances'.

The CRE's propaganda function has if anything been
even more damaging to race relations than its work as an
enforcement agency for the 1976 Act. In the latter role it
has done harm enough by arousing animosity against the
ethnic communities. But, as chief propagandist of the ide-
ology of race equality, it has done even more mischief by
fostering a culture of dependency rather than of self-reliance, aggravated by its constant emphasis on minorities'
rights rather than their obligations.

This negative approach is especially apparent in a CRE
report 'Loading the Law'.[30] It starts by referring to the
decisive part racial injustice played in the riots of 1981,
implying that they were almost justified because blacks
suffered the worst conditions in employment, housing and
education for their children. Racial discrimination is then
said to compound these disadvantages and to launch blacks
on to a 'vicious downward spiral of deprivation'. This
portmanteau phrase seems to be an adaptation of the jargon
from development economics, the 'vicious circle of

poverty' in which many Third World countries are said to be trapped, and it is quite misleading. If the vicious downward spiral of deprivation theory were true, no poor immigrants would ever prosper, though of course we have only to look at the example of Asians in Britain to see that many of them have done remarkably well.

The report then goes on to advocate in the name of equality of opportunity a programme of bestowing economic privileges on the ethnic minorities (which are all lumped together in the report as 'blacks'). As is common form in such publications it ends with a prophecy which is really more of a threat — that if these changes are not adopted there will be further racial violence. It is fair to ask whether violence has not already been stimulated by such perverse propaganda from an official source.

Further insight into this morbid mentality is given in a CRE research report on 'Employment Prospects for Chinese Youth in Britain'.[31] It paints a picture of a narrow inward-looking community interested only in money-making, traditional to a fault, and with the elders tyrannizing over the young who dare not disobey or disagree. Most young Chinese are seen as exploited by their families who put them to work, usually in the family restaurant. There, it is said, they are given a pittance of an allowance rather than a wage and are trapped with little hope of escape; most of them can't speak English well enough to get jobs elsewhere. The traditional attitude of the Chinese towards education is contemptuously described as: 'simple', being summed up as: 'You'll find wealth and beautiful wives in books, so you must study well.' Many of those who are unemployed do not register for benefits because unemployment is seen as a personal failure and would therefore be a disgrace. 'The Chinese ethnic groups, like many others, regard "signing on" and supplementary benefits as stigmatizing.' Further, although 'there are thousands of catering workers within the Chinese community, there is no union to represent their interests. One of the common beliefs within the Chinese community is that they should look after their own relatives and friends and consequently industrial disputes would be rare and in any event soluble between individual employers and employees.' Jobs are obtained largely through the kinship network, especially in Chinatown. If open disputes arise the workers always lose: even if they are successful at a tribunal all jobs on the kinship network will in future be closed to them. The future of the young Chinese is seen as essentially bleak because they are stuck in the catering trade which is contracting. This view is at least questionable in an age of rapid expansion for the service industries, especially those providing for people's leisure.

The pamphlet concludes with a host of recommendations for government involvement with and assistance for Chinese families, including encouragement of young Chinese to apply for work in which, according to the terms of the 1976 Race Relations Act, they are 'under-represented'. Particularly absurd is the principal recommendation that a multi-cultural curriculum should be introduced in every school, 'so that children can learn and can share each other's culture. This will help them to live in our multi-racial society.' It would be hard to conceive of anything less relevant to the needs of the young Chinese than for them to be initiated in, for example, Afro-Caribbean culture. For, even on the pamphlet's own showing, the biggest drawback the Chinese suffer from in this country is their poor knowledge of English.

It is very revealing that this report should convey the idea that these frugal, hard-working, independent and enterprising people are not to be admired but pitied for not knowing or not caring to know how to claim benefits from the welfare state. For it is qualities such as the sense of purpose and perseverance which the Chinese display that are crucial to economic success. The fact that they reject the dependence which the CRE appears to be urging upon them, and prefer to use their own resources or those of their family or community, suggests that they share the attitudes of their brethren in America, who, despite appalling discrimination, have now clambered into the top income brackets. The notion that the prospects for this community are bleak is the reverse of the truth. It is in fact building up the financial and, far more important, human capital which should make its future affluence secure — as long as it resists the blandishments of the CRE.

It is clear that by its constant harping on the racial aspect of everything under the sun, the CRE, instead of improving relations between the races, has made each one of them more conscious of the ways in which it differs from the rest. Thus instead of helping it hinders the racial integration which is its *raison d'être*. A typical example of this is a report which urged that Urdu should be taught to the English in schools. Indeed Urdu, Bengali, Gujerati, Greek, Italian and the other 125 languages spoken by children in British schools should not be treated as 'foreign', said the report. 'They are not foreign languages,' it insisted, 'but languages of the various communities in the United Kingdom.'[32] A similar approach was found in a CRE publication on bias in the subject matter of school lessons.[33] Classes in cookery which didn't include information on Indian and Chinese cuisine were guilty of racial discrimination, it said. Such a statement is a symptom of chronic cultural relativism – the theory that all cultures must always rank the same. This is not to deny that other cultures than our own ought to be treated with anything but respect. But our overriding concern must be with the need of immigrant children to acquire as much knowledge as possible of the customs and behaviour of this country, in which their families have chosen to live, and the priority which must be given to understanding English culture cannot be gainsaid.

Of course, good race relations require not only that the racial minorities adapt to the host community's ways, but that members of the host community adapt to the mores of the minorities. This does not mean that they should demean or humiliate themselves however. Yet how else can one describe the racial awareness courses which the commission is constantly recommending? A report of a seminar on race awareness training[34] published by the CRE argues that the more race-conscious everyone is the better. The object of a race awareness course is to 'produce in participants a heightened awareness of racism in individuals, including themselves and institutions including their own, reinforced by both fact and feeling, sufficient to ferment a determination to resist and actively to confront racism both personally and institutionally and in the wider society'. With all allowances made for gobbledygook it is clear that the object of the courses is to make everybody more or less race-obsessed. The introductory lecturer maintained that the emotions raised by these courses were guilt and anger at 'those responsible' for racism. Yet, though the responsible ones are, as one might expect, the political establishment, the notion that 'we are all guilty' is also associated with the phrase 'institutional racism'. This abject sense of universal culpability is apparently not to be discouraged but fostered. For, 'Although a racial awareness training course might only last for two or three days, it is important that the participants should meet again as a group, reinforce each other, draw support and plan collective action.' Implanting a sense of guilt is of course a very good way of preparing people for manipulation, and the emphasis on group indoctrination rather than the use of individual judgement has a very sinister ring. It hardly needs saying that the cultivation of heightened race awareness, especially when conjoined with a feverish campaign to denounce manifestations of racial prejudice in any form, is ill-calculated to improve race relations but likely to make them febrile, edgy and unstable.

On other policy matters there is a similar attempt to promote the idea that ethnic minorities must be subject to separate consideration and special rules. A CRE pamphlet on housing need among ethnic minorities,[35] and another on racial equality and social policies in London,[36] both stress the 'racial dimension'. There must not only be a policy for the homeless, but a separate and distinct one for homeless blacks. In local government, Principal Race Relations Advisers directly responsible to the Chief Executive should be appointed and 'many other posts', including 'community workers, teachers, librarians, adult educational outreach workers, housing and environmental health workers and interpreters, all of which posts qualify for S11 funding', filled to ensure that the racial dimension is kept in the forefront of the minds of all who have local power. In the case of London boroughs and the Greater London Council in the Ken Livingstone era this injunction needed no repetition but was put into effect at once. And in a later booklet on the Youth Training Scheme[37] the CRE again condemned the general attitude of *laissez-faire* among the authorities. It urged the appointment of specialists in race relations in every region who should report directly to the top man in each case. Their task would be to push at every point for equal opportunities, and, by keeping ethnic records to ensure that ethnics were not 'under-represented', to introduce racial quotas by stealth.

If, then, as I have argued, the CRE has proved a menace to its own objectives of reducing racial discrimination and promoting racial harmony, is this merely the result of inefficiency? Such seemed to be the message, however diplomatically worded, of the Commons Home Affairs Committee in its 1981 report. It found that the commission's chief defect was 'incoherence'. The commission operated without any obvious sense of priorities or any clearly defined objectives. There were few subjects on which they proved unwilling to pronounce and few projects on which they were unwilling to embark. Yet where specific policy objectives were established they were rarely translated into concrete activity.

Commission staff responded to this policy vacuum by setting their own objectives which, not surprisingly, petered out or went off at half cock. The commission in particular showed a 'lamentable inability . . . to produce completed investigations' — it had started forty-five and completed only ten. The reach of the commission's promotional work was, the committee suspected, beyond its grasp. There was also no proper link-up between investigations and promotional activity. In any case, as the MPs were not alone in thinking, there was some doubt as to whether the two functions of pseudo-judicial enquiry and propaganda were compatible. There were other damning detailed criticisms of the commission's competence, the most notable being its handling of the grants financed by the taxpayer with which it funded 'ethnic minority arts' and even one project aimed at 'joy-spreading'.[38]

All this sloppiness might be put down to poor leadership. In this respect the seeds of the CRE's inadequacy were sown at the very start. For, just as Groucho Marx didn't want to join any club that would have him as a member, so no public figure of real consequence, that is with the stature the post was thought to demand, saw the CRE chairmanship as worthy of him. The job was David Steel's for the asking but he didn't feel impelled to ask, happily as it turned out for the Liberal party. Instead it went to an extremely likeable old Etonian Tory MP, David Lane, who had earlier as a junior Home Office minister had race relations as part of his departmental brief. He had the extra advantage, in the eyes of the Labour government then in power, of being one of the Tory 'wets'. That is to say he had a pronounced belief in the power of government action for good. Shortly after he became chairman-designate, he affirmed his faith in political answers to racial questions by declaring, at a press conference convened to launch a pamphlet, 'Cities in Crisis', for the Tory Reform Group, that central government and local authorities should spend at least £100 million a year to tackle the problem of run-down cities. 'Our second-class citizens of 1976,' he commented, 'are hundreds of inner-city dwellers, white and black, who are trapped by urban deprivation.'[39]

Political heavyweight David Lane was not, but, for the task of CRE boss-man, race relations mouthpiece and friendly neighbourhood racial watchdog, he had acquired a tone of voice which was to serve him well in the CRE chair until he was blown out of it by the Home Affairs Committee report.

His place was taken in the summer of 1982 by a tough bureaucrat, Peter Newsam, who had a much less cheery personality than David Lane but did seem to have been better at running the office. It is not apparent however that the CRE's impact on race relations improved. Indeed, since it was set up on a false, and indeed perverse, premise — that intolerance can be cured by law — it would be reasonable to assume that the more efficient the CRE becomes the worse race relations will be.

This may seem a paradox at first, but it is by no means unusual in the history of government regulatory agencies — much of it a tale of bodies set up to protect the public being taken over and perverted by the sectional interests they are meant to administer. In the case of the commission, the process has worked more subtly but to the same effect, for the CRE has been largely usurped by the racial minorities it is supposed to protect. Just how far this process had already gone by the time of Peter Newsam's appointment was shown by the fact, which the Home Affairs Committee also pointed out, that 51 per cent of the commission's staff were either black or Asian hardly their entitlement under a racial quota regime. Such a blatant imbalance has inevitably discredited the CRE and aroused the feelings of hostility it was intended to dissolve. This and other such developments aroused the Home Affairs Committee's alarm and its report was most emphatic:

> One aspect of the commission's style has given rise to particular concern. They sometimes seem to adopt the role of spokesman for what they interpret as the views of ethnic minorities, and to prefer this role to their true one of a quasi-judicial statutory commission. The sub-committee therefore sought and obtained from the commission copies of all their press releases for 1980 and the first six months of 1981. Perusal of these confirmed our impression that the commission are at times unduly eager to engage in instant analysis of current political controversy to the detriment of their main statutory duties and at the cost of the reputation for scrupulous impartiality which many of their functions demand.

It did not help that many of the opinion-formers among the ethnic minorities were genuinely under the impression that the commission was intended to be 'their own institution'.

Many of them certainly behaved as if it was. A CRE booklist about racialism and prejudice in Britain is astonishingly partisan. The books mentioned come largely from bodies like the Runnymede Trust, the Policy Studies Institute and the Institute of Race Relations. They foster the idea that there is a malign conspiracy at work which systematically denies opportunities for ethnic groups to obtain employment, housing, etc. The list makes no pretensions to objectivity and there is no attempt to show that there is another point of view than that of race relations industry personnel.

Again, for a long time the CRE resisted the government proposal in September 1983 to place people who draw the dole into racial groups. Whitehall's object was to provide a picture of the types of people who were unemployed so that government training could help with the right sorts of schemes and language. The CRE's opposition, despite assurances to the contrary, was based on fear that the information might be passed to the Home Office or to immigration officials. The impression given was that the CRE was more on the side of illegal immigrants than of the law.[40]

Another revealing indication of how much the CRE had become identified with the race lobbies was its hostility to the government's proposals in March 1984 for removing from elected local authorities the power to fund ethnic minority groups.[41] This followed the revelation that the Greater London Council had spent £5 million a year to finance minority organizations, and that the ethnic groups among these employed at least 200 community activists. The CRE's warning that, if these people were sacked and sent back to the streets they could provide the focus of future unrest, seemed indicative of the violent nature of these potential activists. The CRE bias also showed itself in its strong support for the continuation of the Inner London Education Authority, and in many of its interventions during the passage of the 1981 Nationality Act, which restricted British citizenship to those with very close ties with the United Kingdom.

Despite such evidence that the commission had subversive influence within the public domain, Mrs Thatcher's government resisted attempts to abolish it. The Prime Minister's predominant feeling was probably that abolition would be more trouble than it was worth, especially when there were more important reforms to be carried out. Perhaps the CRE was regarded as a largely innocuous quango which should be tolerated in order to keep the race relations lobby quiet. Such a view was understandable but unwise. Exactly how subversive the CRE had become and how unregenerate was its ambition to trample on our tradition of freedom under the law is no longer a matter for speculation. It was published for all to see in the form of proposals for changing the Race Relations Act of 1976.[42] First of all it sets out to widen the scope of the act and of course, as a result, the CRE's own authority. As a preliminary it sought to ensure that the principle enshrined in the original act, about which many had the gravest misgivings, should be enforced without demur. This was that to be found guilty of direct discrimination a racial motive does not have to be proved. It went on to redefine indirect discrimination to mean 'significant adverse impact'. In practical terms it sought to impose rather rigid criteria, like a twenty per cent variation from the norm (that is an average share of the community, whatever community is used as marker). Finally it sought to include religious discrimination within the broad definition of illegal race discrimination.

The plain intention of all this redefinition was to reduce the chances of the commission being overruled in court. With the same aim in view various present exemptions from the application of the act would no longer be preserved. Government services previously outside the act's jurisdiction would be included within it. The Immigration Service, on which the CRE has long cast a covetous eye, would fall within the scope of the act, giving the CRE effective control over immigration policy. It would also extend the act to cover people in occupations over which it had formerly held no sway, such as seamen recruited abroad and people working for airlines. In a very ominous move it demanded that, where the act came into conflict with other laws or statutes, it should prevail.

The business of proving discrimination, over which the CRE has had such problems in the past, would under its own proposals become far easier. The presumption that the CRE's alleged transgressor is at fault would be strengthened by adoption of the principle that the accused is guilty unless he or she can prove the contrary. In other words the CRE would introduce the revolutionary principle into English law that the accused is guilty until proven innocent. Refusal to answer a CRE question would also, it was implied, be considered sufficient grounds for assuming guilt. A further innovation would be to set up a discrimination division within another quango to hear both employment and non-employment race and sex discrimination cases. Legal aid would in addition be available for those pursuing race discrimination cases before these tribunals.

As regards its formal investigations and enforcement of the law relating to race relations, present limits on the CRE's freedom of action would be swept away. The commission would have power 'to conduct a formal investigation for any purpose connected with the carrying out of' its duties. Difficulties experienced by the commission in the ordinary courts would vanish under the new arrangements. Formal notices issued by the commission would not be subject to appeal as at present but would go before an independent tribunal — another quango — for examining the facts of the situation. The commission would be given the right to intervene in any proceedings where discrimination was alleged in order to draw the attention of the tribunal to the likelihood of future discrimination in the situation concerned. In the eyes of the average bystander this must look suspiciously like an attempt to bring pressure for a verdict of guilty.

The tribunal would have power to impose mandatory orders on those found guilty of discrimination. Particularly deserving of attention is the proposal that, in educational cases, powers to prescribe changes in teaching practice would be transferred from the Secretary of State for Education to the tribunal. It is depressing to speculate on how, under such an arrangement, Brent headmistress Mrs Maureen McGoldrick would have fared.

The tribunal would have power to award compensation to those suffering from discrimination, and what a power it would be! For first there would be no statutory limit to the amount and second it could take the form of continuing payments until a stipulated event such as a promotion or offer of employment occurred.

In order to speed up the desired changes the commission would be given power to lay down codes of practice not only for employment but in every other area of economic life. Further, it could prescribe ethnic record-keeping in any public employment and housing with the agreement of the Employment Secretary of State. Finally, where there was under-representation in his workforce, an employer would be entitled to favour the members of any ethnic group.

It requires little reflection to perceive that here was an attempt to introduce a universal system of racial quotas in everything but name. This scheme, under the guise of promoting racial equality, would create privileges for racial minorities casuistically justified on the grounds that they would compensate for inequalities which already exist.

This was the programme which the CRE bosses had already mapped out during the long reign of Thatcher and Major. As the introduction indicated, during the Blair era the CRE's ambitions have been in many respects fulfilled. The definition of racial minority has been widened to include religious groups and the Irish. The definition of a racist act as one which is so perceived by the victim or a third party which the Macpherson Report adopted has been imposed upon Britain's police forces with a large resulting leap in apparent racist incidents. Quotas, for jobs etc, under the guise of targets, have been made obligatory in all our public services as have the brainwashing programmes known as race awareness courses. Traditional principles of law which formerly safeguarded the citizen's liberty, such as the presumption of a person's innocence until proved guilty, the right to trial by jury and the prohibition of double jeopardy are in process of being dismantled as enthusiastically recommended especially in the case of race relations cases by Macpherson.

What will be the consequences? Speculation is not called for. Why peer into the crystal when you can read the book? This is the path which the Americans have already trodden — with dire results, as the next chapter shows.

5

American Lessons We Don't Learn

If the essence of intelligence is learning from the trials and errors of others instead of from one's own bitter experience, any enquiry into racial problems over here should take account of what has been happening in that great mongrel republic on the other side of the Atlantic, the United States. For though we are apt to think, like General de Gaulle, that the Americans are predominantly Anglo-Saxon, the truth is that there are almost as many US citizens whose ancestors came from Africa as from Britain. Indeed those of British descent are only fourteen per cent of the whole. The feat of absorbing into one nation people of so many and various immigrant races has been a remarkable one by any standards. Yet it was also a racial issue — the slavery of blacks in the southern states — which brought the one serious threat to America's unity in the two centuries since the founding fathers joined together the original thirteen states.

The integration of blacks into America's social, economic and political order has been a mounting preoccupation ever since. It was in the 1960s, though, that the process came to a head in civil rights marches, inner-city riots and the Great Society programme — an attempt, Promethean in its ambition, to expunge poverty and inequality of opportunity, particularly as it affected blacks, from every corner of the nation's life.

Yet if the relevance of the American experience to our racial problems is obvious enough, the actual lessons it has to offer could hardly have been more thoroughly misunderstood, even, or perhaps especially, among acknowledged experts on the subject. An example of this is Lord Scarman's famous report on the Brixton disorders in 1981. In its conclusion he quoted with enthusiastic approval from an address to the American nation by President Lyndon Johnson in 1968. It was a speech referring to the riots which took place in that year in thirty American cities (which made the Brixton disorders seem trivial in comparison). It went as follows:

> The only genuine long-range solution for what has happened lies in an attack — mounted at every level — upon the conditions that breed despair and violence. All of us know what those conditions are: ignorance, discrimination, slums, poverty, disease, not enough jobs. We should attack these conditions — not because we are frightened by conflict, but because we are fired by conscience. We should attack them because there is simply no other way to achieve a decent and orderly society in America.

Lord Scarman ended with a flourish, 'These words are as true of Britain today as they have been proved by subsequent events to be true of America.'[1]

In fact subsequent events were to show that they were *not* true of America, but at least a part of Lord Scarman's assertion holds up, for they are not true of Britain either. The surprising thing is that, to judge by his bibliography, Lord Scarman appears to have been unaware of the considerable literature of disillusion with the Johnson crusade on behalf of the black poor which had already appeared in America when he produced his report.

One of the early critics to contrast optimistic liberal rhetoric with black lack of progress was Daniel P. Moynihan who, as Assistant Secretary of Labor, had been heavily involved in the Johnson programme. There was also the growing 'Public Choice' school of economists (the leading figure of which, J.M. Buchanan, received the Nobel prize for economics in 1986), which has derided the contemporary idea that governments and their servants are altruists fired by pure benevolence. It is their contention that politicians and bureaucrats are as self-serving as anyone else, in view of which they have constructed a theory of government failure. This is the opposite of the Adam Smith theory of free markets, where each person serving his own enlightened self-interest is guided by an invisible hand to contribute to the good of all. According to the Public Choice doctrine, in the activities of government the pursuit by its servants of their own private purposes (however enlightened) leads through the operations of another invisible hand to unintended and perverse results. These are indeed often the very opposite of those of the policy being pursued.[2]

It is perhaps more remarkable that Lord Scarman should apparently have been unacquainted with the critiques of the Johnson programme from a school of distinguished black American academics. These have various political affiliations but what they have in common is that in their work on poverty they have eschewed wide-ranging indictments of American society and refused to allow the excuse of racial discrimination to become a catch-all explanation applying to every aspect of the plight of the black, especially the urban black, poor.[3] Let us look at the four most important of these academics in turn.

William Julius Wilson, Professor and Chairman of the department of sociology at the University of Chicago, claimed that, as a result of the rapid shift of economic emphasis from the manufacturing to the service sector, success has become increasingly dependent on education. As a result of the famous victories of the civil rights movement over segregation and discrimination in the fifties and sixties, the rewards have increasingly gone to educated blacks. Black college-educated boys and girls have prospered through entering the professions and management.

In other words, the black middle class has markedly improved its position. Meanwhile, however, blacks at the bottom of the heap, the black underclass, the unemployed youths, the single black mothers, the unskilled and the welfare recipients, have slid further back. In such a situation, he argued, it is obvious that race matters less than class.

Walter E. Williams, Professor of Economics at George Mason University, Virginia, took up the same point.[4] He maintains that both blacks and whites, especially the poorer ones, are receiving what amounts to an inadequate education. He supports a voucher system which would allow poor parents to do what the middle classes already do, that is opt out of dud state schools. But what do black leaders say about competition in education? Williams asked the Reverend Jesse Jackson and he replied, 'We shouldn't abandon the public [meaning state] schools.' 'After he said this to me,' says Williams, 'I learned that *he* had abandoned them; he sends *his* children to non-public schools.'

Williams's main theme is that the problems of the black poor are created, not ameliorated, by government. Above all he targets minimum wage laws for the harm they do to poor young blacks. He points out[5] that in earlier times the level of youth unemployment among blacks and whites was the same: by 1976, after minimum wage legislation was passed, black youth unemployment rose to twice that of white youth. This was because employers, being forced to pay a minimum rate, would not take on poorly-qualified workers, among whom there was a disproportionate number of young blacks. Minimum wage laws therefore, though doubtless intended to help the poor black by raising his reward, in practice proved all too often to be the worst kind of race discrimination by pricing him out of a job.

Derrick A. Bell Jnr, Professor of Law at Harvard, sharply criticised school integration policies aiming to produce racial balance in schools, and especially of bussing as the method of achieving them. In his view such policies improved neither mutual understanding between the races nor black academic performance. To make things worse the integrationists talked so much, and often quite unfairly, about the inferior quality of education blacks were getting that it made many whites reluctant to send their children to predominantly black state schools.

The most prolific of this new wave of black intellectuals is Thomas Sowell, Senior Fellow of the Hoover Institution, Stanford University.[6] The breadth of his scholarship is astonishing, comprehending not only the experience of America past and present but that of peoples and cultures the world over, and it is difficult in a limited space to do justice to it. He writes not only eloquently but with searing scorn for what he considers the shoddy arguments of America's race relations industry. This animus is fuelled by the anger he feels towards those who he considers have, through their paternalism, which is a kind of inverted racism (for they make the assumption that non-whites are unable to look after themselves) betrayed his fellow blacks. Instead of liberating them such people have fastened on blacks, especially the poorest of them, a new yoke and forfeited their hope of future improvement. For by increasing black dependence on the public purse, their policies have diminished those qualities of personal responsibility and pride in self-reliance through which alone the black underclass can make good their escape from impoverishment to a better life.

Sowell is caustic about the sloppy thinking behind the assertion that where blacks are worse off than the rest of the community in any respect — whether incomes, jobs, housing or education — that this must be due to racial discrimination. For if this were so, how should one account for the fact that the ethnic groups which come out top of almost every American economic league table are the Japanese, the Chinese and the Jews? For all of these groups were until very recently subject to the most severe discrimination through the law, public hostility or vigilante violence.

To those who riposte that the discrepancy is due to colour prejudice, Sowell points out that there are important differences in economic performance among black groups, whose separateness may not be perceptible to outsiders. For instance, second-generation black West Indians there earn on average higher incomes than Americans of German, Italian, Irish, Polish or Anglo-Saxon ancestry. Again, among indigenous American blacks, the descendants of the pre-Civil War 'free persons of colour' are in almost every respect ahead of their brethren who descended from slaves, and have supplied most of the black leadership in America well into the twentieth century.

Of course Sowell does not dispute that there is unfair discrimination against blacks in America, but he doesn't think that it is crucially important — as long as politicians don't interfere. For in a free labour market, for instance, the anti-black employer is likely to find himself paying higher wages for the privilege, as he sees it, of having all-white labour. He may then be undercut by an employer who is without colour prejudice whose labour costs as a result are lower. Thus competition in a free market discourages racial prejudice. Since the artificial barriers were removed against them in American basketball, black players have fully established themselves. In the American music and entertainment industry, which has recently been comparatively free of race prejudice, the Jews and blacks have prospered for the simple reason that impresarios who let bias against the talented people from these groups influence their recruitment of performers would be at a serious competitive disadvantage.

Those who think that political agitation might cure the malady of racism will find little comfort in the writings of Dr Sowell. As he likes to point out, the Japanese and Chinese Americans who have done so well for themselves have kept out of the nation's politics. The Chinese, indeed, have deliberately kept clear of any political entanglement in the South East Asian countries where they have emigrated, despite all the injustices they have suffered, and have concentrated their energies on economic progress. Sowell says that, craven as this may seem in some eyes, it has undoubtedly paid off.

In contrast those ethnic groups which have sought to improve their condition through politics have, comparatively speaking, fared badly. The American Irish, who have conspicuously engaged in political agitation, have been among the slowest runners of the nineteenth-century European immigrant groups in the prosperity stakes. The American Indians, who have had the longest and closest involvement with the American government, have throughout been stuck economically at the bottom of the class.

Of the million and a half people who claim Indian origin in the USA about half live on or near one of the 260 reservations. Each reservation is independent, with its own system of law, government and leaders. These Indians have enjoyed special status since 1871 when Congress made them wards of state. Now, under twenty different federal programmes, they receive around $3 billion a year purely for being who they are. This includes free medical, hospital, dental and optical treatment and considerable 'tribal payments'. They are provided with free legal services and free education up to PhD level. Those who live on a reservation pay no state or federal taxes whatsoever on land, or income derived from it, nor licence duty on their car. On the reservation they are allowed to sell, for use elsewhere, fireworks which are illegal outside its boundaries. They

are even permitted to fish and hunt without a licence regardless of the seasonal and bag restrictions which apply
to all other Americans, and to sell what they kill. Yet according to American sociologist Ted Williams:

> American Indians have the highest infant mortality rate,
> the shortest life span, the poorest housing, the poorest
> transportation, the lowest *per capita* income, and the low-
> est level of education in the nation. In 1985 the Bureau of
> Indian Affairs reported that the unemployment rate on res-
> ervations had reached 49 per cent. Other sources say it is
> even higher. When last the government checked, approxi-
> mately 400,000 Indians (that is one fourth of the Indian
> population, or 40 per cent of those on reservations) lived
> below the poverty level – more than twice the proportion
> among the general population. No ethnic group in America
> has lower average income than the Indians. Suicide and
> alcoholism are epidemic. The rate of alcohol-related
> deaths among Indians is 5.6 times that of the general popu-
> lation.[7]

The independence of the tribes is jealously preserved, but
this only delivers most of the reservation Indians into the
hands of tyrannical and corrupt tribal leaders who terror-
ize them into submission. So largely as a result of lobby-
ing which took advantage of the American people's sense
of guilt, these Indians have been subjected to 'the twin
burdens of economic socialism and political despotism' and
are the country's most oppressed minority. In 1984 the
mainly Indian Presidential Commission on Indian Reservation Economics concluded in its report that 'One of the
major obstacles to Indian economic progress is the United
States Government.' Its authors spoke with unintended
irony. For the US government, by making them totally dependent on federal assistance and taking away every challenge in their lives has created the biggest possible obstacle to the Indians' economic, or for that matter moral

advance. It is a tragic illustration of the perverse effect of governmental benevolence.[7]

In Sowell's view the argument against seeking economic salvation through politics is that it is so unreliable. In America, 'in broad historical terms, government has changed the rules of the game for blacks in virtually every generation'.[8] Nor has it been possible to rely on the consistency of the Supreme Court which since the Second World War has been helpful to black advancement but throughout most of the nineteenth century was, in the eyes of most observers, cast in the role of implacable enemy of the black cause.

Even apparently disinterested political intervention can be harmful to ethnic minority interests. In the last century, US authorities pressed by social reformers tried to regulate conditions of 'sweatshop' workers who, it was thought, were being exploited. Most of them were immigrants and there was a great concentration of them among the poor Jewish immigrants in New York. In fact, says Sowell, the money thus earned was mostly going into savings and creating the financial base which made it possible for the great mass of the Jewish community in the next generation to move out of the slums.

This is not to say that what ultimately matters for getting on in the world is money. What counts far more is human capital, in the form of skills, education, discipline, capacity for work, adaptability, courage, cheerfulness and good health. Some of these, such as good health, are the result of good luck, though good upbringing may play a part. Other qualities which bear on the ability to produce wealth are sometimes the result of a particular ethnic culture, such as the high regard the Jews have for education, which goes back thousands of years, or their knowledge of urban living, which goes back centuries. In America rural Irish immigrants and blacks from the Deep South have taken three generations to adapt to city life.

The notion that governments can, by throwing enough money at 'ignorance, discrimination, slums, poverty [and] disease', foreshorten the period of assimilation of a particular depressed group is highly doubtful. Politicians who think that they can speed up the process and eliminate differences in economic performance between different ethnic groups by passing laws and making administrative orders requiring affirmative action, not to produce equality of opportunity but equality of result, are set on a dangerous course, as the above criticisms imply. Yet these criticisms, though pertinent, are scattered and diffused and do not convey very specifically just how counter-productive the Lyndon Johnson 'Great Society' programme and its extension under subsequent presidents proved to be. For that we must turn to a remarkable work, *Losing Ground, American Social Policy 1950-1980* by Charles Murray.[9] It traces the course of the 'generous revolution' which produced a twenty-fold expansion of America's welfare provision, and explains how this enormous undertaking, which only really got going in the mid-sixties, far from achieving its priority aim of eradicating poverty among blacks, left them in most respects worse off than before.

It is saddening nowadays to read the rhetoric which accompanied the launch of the modest Kennedy welfare programme of 1962, with its references to giving the poor 'a hand, not a handout'. The assumption then was that, given the training and the opportunity of a job, able-bodied welfare recipients would swiftly be in a position to look after themselves. Unfortunately the dole queue refused to diminish: in late 1967 a White House presidential aide announced that only one per cent of the 7.3 million people on welfare had acquired sufficient skills and training to make them self-sufficient.

So Johnson announced the next stage of the 'battle for

civil rights', that is, 'not just [for] equality as a right and theory but quality as a fact and as a result'. Soon after an executive order required 'affirmative action', meaning deliberate preference in favour of blacks. Let us look at how this new principle performed with regard to poverty, jobs, wages, education, crime and the family.

Poverty

It is generally believed that whatever else the Great Society programme did or did not do it did reduce poverty. In fact there *was* a sharp fall in the numbers below the poverty line, but almost all of it took place before Johnson's programme began. The most telling statistic is for 'latent poverty', that is the number of people who would be poverty-stricken but for government aid. It rose steadily from the late sixties and was unaffected by the seventies boom. This rising population of welfare serfs highlights the failure of the anti-poverty programme because economic independence is crucial to the quality of family life.

Jobs and Wages

From 1965 to 1980 the US federal government spent as much on job-creation as it had spent, in real terms, on the moonshot. Yet this was the very period when black youth unemployment really took off, not only in absolute terms but compared with that of young whites. The figures suggest that young black males especially were flitting in and out of the labour force at the very time when for the sake of their long-term careers they should have been acquiring skills, steady work habits and a good employment record.

The bright side of the picture was that in this period middle-class blacks were breaking through both by obtaining higher-grade jobs (although more than half of them were government posts, doubtless many of them in the anti-poverty programme) and receiving salaries more comparable with whites. Meanwhile, however, the black poor were becoming more than ever stranded in hopeless poverty.

Education

Up until the mid-sixties the education of Americans of all classes was improving. From then until 1980 the gap in educational performance between blacks and whites grew enormously. In 1980 the basic test of recruits' verbal and numerical skills measured by the armed forces showed the white mean score as 2.3 times that of blacks.

Crime

As Murray says, despite their functional illiteracy and lack of skills, young blacks were surviving and one of the ways they were surviving was through crime. Crime rates had been stable until the start of the Great Society programme. It was calculated that, at 1970-levels of homicide, a person living in a large American city had a bigger chance of being murdered than an American soldier in the Second World War of being killed in action. The increase in black arrests for violent crimes during the 1965-80 period was seven times that of whites. Most victims were poor inner-city blacks.

The Family

The original Kennedy welfare plan had as one of its main goals the preservation of the family unit. Yet between the time it was announced and 1980 the black illegitimate birthrate rose from 23 per cent to 48 per cent of the total, while among black teenagers the illegitimacy rate was approaching 100 per cent. Naturally the number of black households with female heads rose sharply. This is important because experience suggests that the members of such households tend to be poor. Indeed the statistics show that in 1980 two-thirds of all poor blacks were living in families headed by a single female.

The popular, as opposed to liberal establishment wisdom in America was that such evidence showed that welfare made people lazy, that soft judges encouraged crime and that there were too many schools devoting their energies to bussing kids instead of teaching them to read. So prevalent did these views become that progressives found it necessary to disprove them. At the Office of Equal Opportunities in Washington they therefore started an experiment involving 8,700 people over a ten-year period, to show that guaranteeing people an income does not turn them into layabouts. In fact it proved, in so far as any social experiment can prove anything, that the assumptions of the federal bureaucrats and their advisers were resoundingly wrong, while completely vindicating the commonsense of the man in the street. Both whites and blacks in the sample did considerably less work while there was a particularly disastrous impact on black family life. The family break-up of the generally poorer Spanish-speaking members of the group was even more calamitous.

It must be emphasized that, in producing this evidence of growing poverty, unemployment, crime, illegitimacy and so on, Murray is not trying to mount a moral indictment of the American blacks. On the contrary he sees them as victims of a policy of 'affirmative' action which, ironically, its proponents regard as the acme of anti-racism. In Murray's and this author's view it is the advocates of the policy who should be indicted. They should be charged with creating, by negligence and wilful refusal to recognize the facts of human nature, a welfare system which promised to make the condition of the black poor better but has instead made it substantially worse.

Murray is saying no more about the American blacks than that they respond to economic incentives like everybody else. The rules were such that young couples were encouraged to live together while remaining unmarried. The rules also encouraged the man not so much to stay in a state of permanent unemployment but to move in and out of the job market. This tendency towards periodic rather than steady employment was especially harmful to the long-term interests of young black males, who were dropping in and out of dead-end jobs and failing to establish either regular work habits or the kind of work record which would help them when they were seeking better, higher-paid jobs later on.

Similarly counter-productive was a rule introduced late in the programme which allowed women to earn $30 without loss of welfare benefit and thereafter to keep two-thirds of any earnings without losing it. Intended to encourage women on welfare to get a job, it actually had the effect of inducing many more working women, who had previously been independent, to go on welfare. This growth in the army of dependants was greeted with perverse delight by many welfare enthusiasts as evidence of how the 'stigma' of being on welfare was being removed, so that people were now claiming federal handouts not as a privilege but as a right.

Those doing less work had more time for crime, but the main reason why the Great Society programme coincided with an explosion of criminal violence and theft is that, for the average murderer, mugger, rapist and robber, deterrents were reduced while incentives increased. From the sixties to the mid-seventies the chances of evildoers being caught, or if caught punished, rapidly declined. In the big cities the judges were strongly influenced by the idea that crime is a response to exploitation and poverty so that deterrence doesn't work. Their compassionate approach to sentencing, especially for crimes by the young, yielded a rich harvest of juvenile delinquency. Meanwhile restrictions on access to court and criminal records of juveniles proved a great boon to youthful offenders.

The same indulgent official attitudes towards misbehaviour in the young in the large urban schools had parallel consequences. Schools which favoured a white middle-class approach towards education and went in for such punishments as suspension and expulsion could soon be brought to heel by being denied federal funds for discriminating on grounds of race. If the school persisted in its old-fashioned ways and tried to maintain academic standards by making students reattempt grades they hadn't passed, the teachers and administrators had to run the gauntlet of court cases brought by pupils or their parents accusing them of infringing their civil rights. Good teachers and good pupils were discouraged while the rebellious and disruptive pupils were let off lightly. No wonder there was a decline in the proportion of schoolchildren who could read, write and count.

Practically all the incentives of the welfare system thus pointed in the same negative direction while each one tended to reinforce the others. As Murray said,

> It was easier to get along without a job. It was easier for a man to have a baby without being responsible for it, for a woman to have a baby without having a husband. It was easier to get away with crime. Because it was easier for others to get away with crime it was easier to obtain drugs. Because it was easier to get away with crime it was easier to support a drug habit. Because it was easier to get along without a job it was easier to ignore education. Because it was easier to get along without a job, it was easier to walk

away from a job and thereby accumulate a record as an unreliable employee.

It is indeed a case of being trapped in a cycle of deprivation, but not the kind usually attributed by progressives to capitalism. On the contrary it is the ironic result of a public welfare system originally designed to rescue the poor, especially the black poor, from their depressed condition and to give them dignity and independence.

But, says Murray, it was not just a matter of the black poor being given incentives to act against their own long-term interests. The situation was further aggravated by withdrawal of the status rewards for the kind of *positive* behaviour which would enable them to escape to a better life. Once the authorities conceived the view that the poor were not responsible for their condition because 'the system is to blame', then the distinction between the deserving and the undeserving poor disappeared. The poor were all bracketed together as helpless people whose only hope was to be rescued by their betters. Striving and the proud boast of not taking charity from anyone were things of the past, a mug's game when everyone was on the take and welfare an automatic right. Indeed many welfare programmes made failure a condition of eligibility. The old role models, the boys who heroically worked their way up and out of the ghetto through night school and scholarships, were no longer admired but accused of 'acting white', and treated as outcasts or worse.

Murray's book, which was called the Reagan administration's new bible, concludes that the principles of social action to help the poor must be revised. It is no good treating the laid-off worker in the same way as the drone. It is wrong to put the law-abiding on the same basis as the delinquent. We must be wary of robbing Peter to pay Paul because all transfers tend to be treacherous — what looks like a transfer from rich to poor all too often turns out to be taking from one poor group to give to another. We should handle transfers with the same caution as dangerous drugs — avoid their use unless we are confident that it will add to the world's net happiness: not at all an easy thing to assess.

We had best face the fact that any social reform is of its nature likely to be flawed. If we set up a programme to help poor black criminals, drug addicts, unemployables or illiterates, we at the same time create a demand, and very likely end up offering rewards for being criminals, drug addicts, unemployables or illiterates. A reform which is intended to bring about a change in human behaviour is likely to succeed only if it goes with the grain of human nature. Otherwise it is likely to do more harm than good. The more difficult the problem the more damage it is likely to do.

Judged by these criteria Murray contends that the American social programmes beginning in the last half of the sixties subjected the black poor to new forms of racism worse in their results than the old ones which they were supposed to offset. And he concludes, 'My proposal for dealing with the racial issue in social welfare is to repeal every bit of social legislation and reverse every court decision that in any way requires, recommends or awards differential treatment according to race.'

This is the conclusion of one of America's leading experts about the American Great Society experiment of preferential treatment of racial minorities which has been given the name of 'affirmative action', and which well-intentioned reformers like Lord Scarman and the rather more interested parties associated with the Commission of Racial Equality would have us adopt in Britain.

The conclusion is that, even though it was backed by the resources of the world's biggest and richest democracy, the experiment was a gigantic flop. Not only did it fail to advance the cause and condition of the blacks and the other depressed racial minorities, it actively harmed them. The best thing to do next is to go back to square one.

That is what many Reagan supporters were hoping would happen when he first arrived in the White House. Their disappointment has been eloquently described by David Stockman, the Director of the Office of Management and Budget for four and a half years.[10] He and the other 'supply-siders' were eager to unleash the energies of the American people and through the incentive of tax cuts start a new era of economic growth. But for this to be really effective there had to be corresponding and simultaneous expenditure curbs. Reagan did carry out the largest tax reductions in history but the parallel curtailment of spending never took place. Stockman had singled out the welfare programmes for the largest cuts but their figures obstinately refused to shrink. The Social Insurance and Poverty programme, which absorbed 9.6 per cent of Gross National Product in 1980, was still absorbing 9.5 per cent in 1986. Why did the government falter and the pressure groups succeed?

Stuart M. Butler, Director of Policy Studies at the Heritage Foundation, has recently addressed the question of why conservatives were unable to enlist support for this reform despite the clear failure of the Great Society to eliminate poverty, its primary goal.[11] He claims that first it was because the conservatives did not explain in easily understandable terms why the Great Society welfare state was incapable of erasing poverty. Second, they did not convey a convincing picture of what they would put in its place. Lyndon Johnson's war on poverty, faulty as it proved, at least captured the public imagination.

To start with, let us look at the reasons why the Johnson poverty programme failed so dramatically. First, it was a one-way obligation. The poor were assumed to have an automatic right to welfare but no associated duties. The system was so organized that people were trapped in a state of dependency from which they could not escape.

Second, it was a highly centralized system with, as a result, inflexible rules and standardized assistance packages instead of what was needed — a flexible response to individual needs. This left little scope for local discretion and fresh ideas.

Third, the poor were not able to choose between alternative suppliers of the services they were given. Professional intermediaries such as teachers and social workers chose for them. 'That,' says Butler,

> is why we have public high schools in America where the children cannot read and yet the teachers never have to face competency tests; it is why we have squalid public-housing projects and welfare hotels with prosperous managers; and it is why many adoption services incarcerate children in institutions, drawing thousands of dollars a year in management fees, rather than place a child with a family and lose their government grant.

From this diagnosis emerges an alternative vision of welfare. Instead of a 'free-lunch system' there would be a '*workfare* system'. Rather than being simply entitled to government hand-outs their recipients would either train or perform whatever work they can. Individuals would have to take responsibility for their dependants. If a teenage boy fathers a child he should be obliged to support it through his job or public sector work; if he refuses he should be jailed.

Again, parents should be responsible for the actions of their children, as in the state of Wisconsin. There the parents of any teenager who becomes a parent must contribute towards any welfare assistance provided by the state. Priority concern for the innocent child should mean that welfare payments do not encourage unmarried teenage mothers to get up an 'independent' household where she and the child are condemned to a lifetime of unemployment and welfare dependency. In short the aim is to strengthen by all possible means the principle of self-help.

Next, welfare must be decentralized from the government to what Glenn C. Loury, professor of political economy at Harvard, calls 'mediating structures'[12] which stand between the individual and public authority, such as the family, church associations and other private bodies. The traditional family's role as the bulwark against poverty should be encouraged, especially since the scourge of child poverty is concentrated in families with one parent not two.

As far as possible neighbourhood welfare arrangements should take the place of national welfare arrangements. Everyone has a structure of loyalties, with the family normally coming first, then the local community, extending outward in a series of widening and weakening circles to the nation. The closer, more immediate and more familiar the influence, the stronger and more sympathetic the bond. By experimenting with schemes involving different combinations of these loyalties, welfare should not only be decentralized but diversified.

Finally, the stranglehold of the professional service suppliers must be broken by giving the power of choice to the welfare poor. Instead of the teachers having control of the children's education, vouchers should transfer it to parent power. Similarly, efficient, convenient and economical public housing is found where tenants take over the management themselves.

A welfare system on these lines would reinforce the social structure instead of destroying it as the present one has tended to do. Stuart Butler is harking back to Churchill's commonsensical attitude to welfare — that it should be a springboard, not a featherbed. It is an approach which, if applied to Britain's welfare services, could, from the ethnic minorities' point of view have admirable results.

6

Scarman and the Riots

Britain in the 1980s was the scene of race-related riots and urban disorder unprecedented in modern times. For the British public the spectacle, made vivid by TV, of ferocious mobs of largely black youths, not in just one but several cities, engaging in pitched battles with the police was traumatic indeed. For a people grown complacent in the assumption that this sort of thing only happened abroad, it was shattering. The knowledge that, in these conflicts, hundreds of policemen were injured and that in 1985 in the Tottenham riots on the Broadwater Farm Estate Police Constable Blakelock was murdered, generated countrywide alarm.

Far from taking some responsibility for the disaster upon themselves the race relations professionals rose up and denounced British society with even greater vehemence than before. For them these disorders were the condign rewards of endemic racism among the white majority. And, if the original natives of these islands stood accused, so in even greater measure did those who were officially deputed to act on their behalf. The police were portrayed not as law and order's front line of defence but as white supremacists, agents of oppression and exponents of brutal tactics intended to provoke.

Thus the 1985 Annual Report of the Commission for Racial Equality, stated: 'Most of those directly involved, in many cases as victims, were black. Most of those involved in suppressing the riots, in commenting on them or simply watching them on their television screens, were white.'[1] Note the suggestion that blacks were 'victims' even though they were the people doing the rioting and as if there were no victims among the police. Note too the implication that the white majority was somehow at fault purely on the grounds that they were watching the riots on television. For it is hardly remarkable that the commentators were largely white; they would have to be, given their weight in the total population, even on a quota basis. Only people who are paranoid about race could lump together facts of this kind and read racist oppression into them. Rarely has the widespread suspicion that those whose profession it is to combat racial conflict have a vested interest in promoting it been more convincingly displayed.

The real danger of such an approach, however, lay not in its expression by bureaucrats of the race relations industry but in its adoption by a British law lord in an official report on the Brixton riots. The moderate tone and judicious language of Lord Scarman should not deceive anyone into believing that his report was impartial. Predictably it has become the bible of the race relations lobby, providing a fund of authoritative-sounding quotations to justify all manner and variety of mischievous and costly public intervention.

In the first instance Scarman's remit was to enquire into the inadequacies of policing which had led to the riots in Brixton (later widened to include the disturbances in Southall, Toxteth and Moss Side and the West Midlands). The noble lord then requested that his terms of reference should be broadened to include the social and economic causes as well. It is no reflection on his integrity but a recognition of his general cast of mind to say that the broad shape of Lord Scarman's conclusions was predictable from the word go. His investigation, naturally, required him to demand evidence from all the interested parties. The marker for the race relations lobby was put down by the Commission for Racial Equality. Its evidence, its main line of reasoning and many of its demands, though not its hectoring tone, provide much of the stuff of the eventual report.

The CRE's submission was indeed a disagreeably complacent document, developing the 'You should have listened to us before' theme and making copious use of its own previous publications, a little more attention to which, it claimed, would have enabled the authorities to nip the riots in the bud. 'A disregard of previous reports and recommendations,' it says, 'was a significant contributory factor in Brixton.' An unfortunate reference came near the end of the submission in what was clearly intended to be a withering attack on the failure of the authorities to learn from the earlier social disorders in American cities. It cited the refusal to take on board or to benefit from the work of the Kerner Commission, set up to investigate the causes of America's riots in 1968. According to John O'Sullivan, a former *Daily Telegraph* staffer by then editing a Republican political quarterly, *Policy Review*, in Washington, the citation of Kerner as an authority on civil disorders was the source of amazement among newspapers over there. For the report was as discredited as its author, Otto Kerner, who was later convicted of bribery, income tax evasion, perjury, conspiracy and mail fraud. The Kerner Report had concluded that the riots were caused by 'white racism', black poverty and powerlessness. It also arrived at the sensational conclusion that the black rioter was, in O'Sullivan's words 'a most superior person, better-educated and more politically committed than the dull and self-effacing non-rioter'.[2] Yet in fact, as O'Sullivan pointed out, both these conclusions had been shot down. Kerner had not been able to show any causal link between the riots and black grievances. The riots had occurred in parts of America where blacks were relatively well treated. The studies of both arrested and non-arrested rioters showed that the rioters had no more grievances than the others and both groups felt that they had made substantial economic progress. As for the alleged superior education of those who had rioted, this was apparently based on a statistical error.

It is not surprising that the CRE should have been beguiled by the Kerner Report or tried to market its 'lessons', since these tune in so harmoniously with its own views. These views were (and are) much as one would expect of a mouthpiece of the ethnic minorities, which, as has been pointed out earlier, is what the CRE has become. Of course the CRE will deny this, but it is surely evident in the fact that, apart from one introductory comment to the effect that police/community relations are a two-way street, the whole emphasis of its submission to Scarman was on what public bodies could do for blacks, with scarce a mention of what blacks could themselves contribute to improved race relations. Indeed, in the list of recommendations, there was no suggestion that the black minority had any duties at all.

As for the CRE's recommendations, they consisted of a whole range of proposals for removing racial disadvantage, which predictably amounted to the conferring of special privileges on ethnic minorities — the nostrums they had been peddling for years. In the important opening section concerning what central government should do, the CRE called for changes in the law to give the ethnics greater protection, monitoring of racial disadvantage (implying a policy of covert racial quotas), more government money and administrative action to support ethnic 'needs' in respect of employment, housing, training and business loans. Other recommendations followed covering yet more areas of policy, demanding that blacks be given further rights and financial assistance. More significant was the section dealing with the police, for out of nine proposals in this section Scarman adopted six. These were:

• Improved community policing techniques.

- Screening out of racially prejudiced police recruits.

- Racism-awareness training sessions for the police.

- More and more effective community liaison staff to be employed.

- Direct and constant dialogue between the police and members of the black community.

In pointing this out I am not trying to suggest that Lord Scarman was a pushover for the CRE. The more likely explanation is that the CRE, which had been developing programmes of self-aggrandizement for years, was ready and waiting when the call for changes came following the Brixton troubles. To some this might appear to be democracy at work, but it is more to the point to see it as the classic process by which quangos grow. The CRE, as we have seen, was the last of a series of race relations bodies appointed by central government to smooth out race relations at times when they were getting rough, and also to demonstrate that the government of the time was 'doing something' about the politically contentious matter of race. It was soon hijacked by the ethnic minorities it was supposed magisterially and benevolently to oversee, and has consistently sought to magnify its own authority and extend the power of those who claim to give racial minorities a lead. When a crisis occurs in a racially mixed area, CRE pooh-bahs are inevitably appointed expert witnesses before another quango — a judicial enquiry; for this second, short-lived quango is established principally to damp down passions and can hardly help taking seriously the 'specialists' from the semi-governmental body intended to supervise race relations. The 'specialists''evidence therefore has a great influence on the final report. Later the police come under pressure to show they are responding to its recommendations. The result of this is that, in effect, those who have been attacking the police end up having a big say in their reform.

The Scarman Report has exerted a profound influence on the content and form of public argument over race and disorder ever since. By its conclusion that the conflict was 'neither premeditated nor planned' but 'erupted from the spontaneous reaction of crowds to what they believed to be police harassment', prime responsibility for the riot was removed from the rioters. Although the report did refer to a 'sinister contribution' of strangers rioting and distributing petrol bombs, this was mentioned only to be dismissed. For all its qualifications, and the Scarman Report contains a great many, the blame in the end falls first on the police, against whom there was 'an outburst of anger and resentment by young black people', and second on underlying social conditions. It followed that, if the police were at least partly to blame, it was necessary for them to reform their ways. That called for new policies in police recruitment, training, methods, monitoring and discipline. It should be understood throughout the force, said the report, that the normal penalty for racially prejudiced behaviour is dismissal. Policing in the racially mixed inner cities should be 'sensitive'. Scarman was particularly critical of such 'insensitive' operations as 'saturation' policing, stop-and-search operations and (the use of) units like the Special Patrol Group. There should be an independent complaints procedure and, though Scarman rejected local authority control of the police, obligatory consultation with local authorities on a continuous basis.

While very properly insisting that the law should be the same for everyone, Scarman's recommendations essentially amounted to the police pursuing a softly-softly policy in racially sensitive areas. Well might the average Bobby on the beat be bemused by Scarman's abjuration to be not merely 'firm' about applying the law but 'imaginative' as well.

Yet, important as this 'reform' of the police has been, the main thrust of the Scarman Report was straightforwardly political. Ultimately the noble lord was far less concerned about police misconduct than about the political attitudes which determined the 'underlying conditions' of the ethnic groups. He plainly did not expect the necessary changes to be brought about by any efforts by members of the ethnic community themselves. The report finally translated into a call for intervention by a paternalist state. The prescription was based on Lord Scarman's observation that Brixton, with its black population of 36 per cent, suffered in extreme form from the social problems and general deprivation common to inner-city areas. These were:

- Severe housing problems and lack of adequate leisure and recreational facilities.

- Family problems, with a high proportion of one-parent households. (The majority of children in care in the wards where the riots took place were black.)

- Under-achievement by many West Indian children in Brixton and failure to acquire the language, culture and skills needed to obtain employment, despite much dedicated work in the schools.

- The higher and also longer lasting unemployment of blacks in the area to a great extent caused by employers' discrimination.

While Lord Scarman did not excuse young blacks of Brixton from responsibility to uphold public order he did not, to judge from this litany of their misfortunes, appear to believe that they had much responsibility for their 'underlying conditions'. The implication of his diagnosis was that only the authorities could materially improve their position. His report was indeed an indictment of the alleged injustice and inefficiency of Britain's law enforcement regime and of the public social provisions for racial minorities, with political action offering the only means through which these defects could be redeemed. It was the judgement of a powerful mind which nevertheless, despite appearances, ignored more than it illuminated.

Scarman's main conclusion, that the Brixton riot was spontaneous, is open to doubt. BBC Television was warned of the riot by a phone call two hours in advance. Large groups of black youths were forming beforehand while various whites with cameras were photographing every move the police made. A number of left-wing agitators were recognized in the mob. Some helped to make Molotov cocktails, which, together with iron bars, were available in suspiciously large quantities.[3] These facts suggest that, far from erupting spontaneously, the riot was planned in advance by people who were manipulating Brixton's black youth in an attempt to destabilize this country's democratic society.

As regards the conduct of the police, on Scarman's own showing one of their main failures in Brixton was not to quell the riot as soon as it began. At least in this respect the policing at the time of the disturbances was not excessively harsh but not harsh enough. In fairness it should be said that Scarman's strictures were levelled against the saturation policing of the area prior to the outbreak in the so-called 'Operation Swamp', which amounted to provocation. Yet this operation was mounted in response to keen local concern over the high level of muggings and other street crimes. The alternative was for the police to accept in practice that, where communities are hostile, no-go areas are an inevitable fact of life. It was all very well for Lord Scarman to deny this and to argue that the real alternative was and is greater police/community cooperation. For where such co-operation did not spontaneously occur, as in the borough of Lambeth, the police, if they had simply allowed the street gangs to carry on mugging, would have failed in their primary task. As a result of Scarman's report, however, the attitude of the authorities towards black law-breakers became less firm.

Nor was the situation improved by the broken-backed way in which the law finally dealt with the culprits. Although 292 Brixton rioters were arrested, a month later only a third had been processed by the courts and not one of the arrested had been sent to gaol.[4] One phrase in the Scarman Report which lingers in the mind occurs in his description of young rioters who 'found a ferocious delight in their activities'. This parallels what was remarked upon by Professor Banfield of Harvard University in his book *The Heavenly City* in a chapter entitled 'Rioting Mainly for Fun and Profit'. There he argued that riots, instead of expressing some general resentment or sense of political injustice, were only examples of 'animal spirits and of stealing by slum-dwellers, mostly boys and young men'. A potent factor in their behaviour, he argued, was the realization that they had little to fear from the police and the courts. Police, under threat from civil rights legislation if they put a foot wrong, tended to look the other way when blacks committed crimes. The courts, influenced by progressive sociologists, tended increasingly not to enforce the law against offenders who were young, poor and black.

John O'Sullivan's article, already referred to,[5] also cites the analysis of Miss Midge Decter in a feature in the American magazine *Commentary,* about the New York looting.[6] She said that their elders and betters in the liberal establishment had been telling young blacks for years in newspapers, magazines, TV and radio 'that they are inherently and by virtue of their race inferior. They must not be judged by the standards which apply to everyone else . . . It is, to be blunt about it, the message of liberal racism. As for the idea that stopping a riot by using enough force to crush it is mere tinkering with the problem and that it is necessary to deal with the underlying social causes, O'Sullivan quotes the riposte of Professor Van Den Haag: 'This view suggests a fireman who declines fire-extinguishing apparatus by pointing out that "in the long run only the elimination of the causes of fire can make a significant and lasting difference . . ." Firemen who behaved like this would, rightly, be accused of passing the buck.' Talk of underlying causes is no excuse. Some causes of conflict are hundreds of years old like the Catholic versus Protestant enmity in Ulster, the Walloon versus Fleming struggle in Belgium, or the clash between French- and English-speaking people in Quebec. The solution of these stubborn problems is not something we can afford to argue about while failing to suppress the violence they cause.

In a brilliantly perceptive article the *Economist* also scorned the idea that the Brixton troubles derived from a sudden explosion of black wrath. It doubted whether there was any generalized cause for riots: '. . . hooligan disorders periodically break out in summer in most big world cities. . . . A particular law or careless act of policing upsets the normal pattern of local order and triggers violence.' It pointed out that ever since the Notting Hill riots in 1958, parts of most British cities have seen periodic outbursts of aggression usually against the police and selected properties (mostly derelict or abandoned). It claimed that there was no central motivation in the Brixton riots apart from young blacks being angered by what they considered to be discriminatory policing. Disorders spread because whites as well as blacks saw on television how easy it was to get away with looting.

If the riots had really been protests against

unemployment, why had they not appeared in Glasgow and Tyneside where the level of unemployment is among the country's highest and most prolonged? Nor is it necessary to be unemployed in order to riot, as white British football fans have demonstrated all over Europe. The worst riots of the seventies were among blacks whose unemployment level was lower than that of blacks elsewhere in Britain who were quiescent. Again, if the riots were really a protest against lack of government support for deprived areas, why did they break out in Toxteth, which had received more government financial help over the previous decade than almost any other district in Britain?[7]

The reaction to the Brixton riots was thus an extreme example of falsely attributing local events to cosmic causes and particular problems to general grievances. At the time Andrew Alexander in the *Daily Mail* attacked attempts to explain the Brixton riots as the result of the number of blacks out of work.[8] Why, he asked, if the length of the dole queues determined the degree of disorder was Northern Ireland, where they were longer than anywhere else, at the time comparatively peaceful? As he went on to add, when the Ulster troubles had been at their height, the British press produced a quite different set of explanations for the unrest. Then it was said that the marchers were angry about denial of civil rights, or, more specifically, unfairness in the allocation of council houses and limitations on the franchise in council elections. Yet when the Protestant ascendancy was ended and these injustices removed, the troubles did not end any more than, Alexander predicted, the disturbances in Brixton would cease when unemployment was reduced. His belief was that the root of the trouble in both Ireland and Brixton lay in people who wanted to undermine the political system. They knew that if marchers came into conflict with the police this could prompt a reaction which some would dub 'police brutality'. Official enquiries could then be demanded and acceded to which by criticizing the police might reduce police morale, thus taking the opponents of our political system closer to their ultimate objective of overthrowing it. Undoubtedly this is another generalized explanation but it is more convincing than Scarman's determinism, according to which, given bad social and economic conditions, riots inevitably erupt.

There is little doubt that the police sought in good faith to carry out the bulk of the recommendations of the Scarman Report regarding recruitment, training, community liaison and consultation in a genuine attempt to diminish racial animosity against them. Nor was this policy a flash in the pan in the immediate aftermath of the riots. The political pressure to expunge racism from the police was maintained after the departure of Whitelaw to the Lords and the arrival at the Home Office of Leon Brittan. In May 1984, for instance, Brittan issued a directive to the Metropolitan Police Commissioner and the forty-two chief constables of England and Wales to keep records of all officers disciplined for all matters involving racism. This policy had in fact already been started the previous January following a critical report by the Policy Studies Institute'[9] which had been ordered by the Metropolitan Police Commissioner at the time, Sir David McNee, just before he retired. It found, after three years' study, that the police force was deeply infiltrated by racial prejudice and racist talk. To the enquirers one source of 'serious concern' was that young men of West Indian origin had the highest chance of being stopped by the police. Yet if the chances of their being stopped by the police were the same as those of the rest of the population there would have been cause for more serious concern, for crime rates for West Indians were, in proportion to their numbers, very high indeed. This fact was clear from figures issued by Scotland Yard in March 1983 which showed that, in the previous year, of 19,258 muggings reported in London, 10,960 were committed by blacks.

Of course it is true that the identification of muggers as black may not always be accurate as many of the muggings take place in the dark. The evidence, however, of a research report in September 1984 which investigated the number of black prisoners in British gaols was not open to this criticism as their colour could be verified by daylight. What it showed was that, in the south east of England, whereas young whites outnumber young blacks by thirty to one in the population as a whole, in youth custody centres the ratio was only three to one. The term 'blacks' was not used in the report in order to distinguish between West Indians and Asians, who are often inaccurately lumped into this general category. In fact, though in the population as a whole Asians numbered one in thirty, in the prisons they were one in seventy, that is they were far less prone to crime (or at least to going to prison for it) than the rest of the nation.[10] This undeniable evidence does show that there is a hugely disproportionate number of blacks sentenced for crimes, and the clear implication is that they commit more crimes.

The disproportionate amount of crime committed by West Indians would account for another conclusion of the report, perhaps disturbing at first sight, namely that the West Indians have substantially more than average contact with the police as offenders and suspects. Nevertheless the police took the report's conclusion seriously and sought ways of reducing racial prejudice in the force. That positive results could be achieved was shown in the matter of racial attacks. The House of Commons Home Affairs Committee criticized the low clear-up rate of this crime — only 13 per cent in 1984 and 15 per cent in 1985 — in the Metropolitan area compared with 64 per cent in Avon and Somerset. Yet in one Metropolitan borough, Tower Hamlets, the record palpably improved. There the police had local training, put more constables on the beat, had a twenty-four-hour helpline, used local volunteers from the Bangladeshi community, established a multi-agency forum for discussing cases and gained local confidence with a commitment to firm action. As a result the clear-up rate rose from 8 per cent in 1984 to 31 per cent in 1985.[11]

As well as attempting to induce the police to follow the recommendations of the Scarman Report, the government also accepted an amendment to its Criminal Justice Bill from peers led by Lord Scarman to make racial discrimination by police officers a criminal offence. His Lordship had urged the change, saying that no single step could be more effective in building up black people's confidence in the police.'[12]

A strongly contrasting view was put by Sir Eldon Griffiths, then a Tory MP and parliamentary adviser to the Police Federation, who gave a friendly but serious warning about police morale. 'I have not known a time,' he said, 'when the police have felt so let down by their friends,' and added that they had been 'astounded' that the government should lend its authority to such an amendment when they were under attack from stones and petrol bombs and from the rear in Labour-controlled authorities.[13] He further remarked in an article in the *Daily Express* that while Parliament was debating the Police and Criminal Evidence Act, the Greater London Council spent more than a million pounds on publicity which portrayed the police as racist oppressors. In support of this contention he referred to a pamphlet issued by certain GLC-financed women's organizations which suggested that white doctors, backed. by the police, would use contraceptive jabs available through the National Health Service to 'solve the immigrant problem' by rendering black females infertile. He summed the position up as follows: 'A powerful combination of the civil liberties and race relations industries, local politicians, pundits and the know-it-alls of TV have been guaranteed to hold the police — not the rampaging youths — responsible for racial clashes.'[14]

The government and the police authorities thus made a real and sustained attempt to reduce all manifestations of racism in the force. Whether these urgings always had the desired effect on the constabulary is more open to doubt. To the man on the beat the race issue was one more complication in a task which was difficult enough in a period of rising crime. Monitoring racism, like monitoring anything else, meant more form-filling and bureaucracy. There was bound to be resentment among the rank and file at the extra burden and at the constant need, where ethnic suspects were concerned, to watch their step. One small grievance was a report that the police in Brixton should not, while on duty, wear a tie commemorating recent riot operations in the borough as it was thought to be in bad taste and likely to provoke ill-feeling. More ominous were the words of the Metropolitan Police Commissioner, Sir Kenneth Newman, following a visit to the 'front line' in Brixton soon after his appointment. In a solemn and considered statement he said: 'They are being spat upon. They are being gratuitously abused. They are having things thrown at them for no reason at all. And there are attempts to trap them into ambushes.'[15] This came from an officer who was as committed to 'sensitive' policing in multi-racial areas as anyone and who, having just come from service in Ulster, knew a thing or two about riots. He recognized the danger-signals of a situation where the police were showing all the 'sensitivity' while, from the population it was protecting, indifference or sullen hostility was the only response.

On the whole the police have always accepted that

misrepresentation and implacable enmity from political and intellectual radicals are an occupational hazard. Against that they have had better pay and conditions after the arrival in power of Mrs Thatcher. But they were ill-prepared for the systematic anti-police propaganda which has for some years now not merely been purveyed but *financed* by left-wing local authorities whose sympathies are often openly with those who break rather than with those who enforce the law.

Baroness Cox, who has done valuable work exposing the deliberate left-wing bias introduced into the state schooling sector has become increasingly incensed at the way teenagers in inner-city schools are being urged to re-sent the police. An example of the sort of subversive lit-erature she had in mind was a glossy cartoon book issued by the Institute of Race Relations on 'How Racism Came to Britain'. Written for youngsters of ten and upwards, 'it is crammed with pictures of Britain as a crude colonial power exclusively concerned with greed and profits. It as-serts that British opposition to slavery was really motivated not by Christian principles — so much for Wilberforce — but by richer pickings elsewhere.'

More central to our purpose here was a video produced by the GLC and, of course, financed by the ratepayer, called 'Policing London' in which the Communist *Morning Star* figures prominently. 'Grossly one-sided, it shows the po-lice as idle, insensitive, blatantly racist, callously indiffer-ent to attacks on women and behaving improperly on a picket-line [thus appealing to] a ragbag of causes.'[16] There were photographs of police manhandling a little boy. A pic-ture of two policemen arresting a young man covered with blood was headed 'A Search for Excitement'. There was no attempt to show that the police had taken criticism of themselves seriously and that the Metropolitan Police Com-missioner had recently issued a 'Guidance for Professional

Behaviour'.

On Sunday 8 September 1985 it was carnival time in the racially mixed Handsworth district of Birmingham and the festivities were launched by no other than the city's Chief Constable. Yet many of those who were happily dancing to steel bands that evening were, twenty-four hours later, dancing round the flames of a neighbourhood on fire. The whole thing began with a trivial incident when a Rastafarian motorist was challenged by a policeman over his vehicle's out-of-date licence. When eventually the policeman attempted to arrest the driver over a hundred black youths appeared and he and colleagues who had subsequently joined him came under attack. This was the start of a full-scale riot in the course of which the police suffered heavy casualties, dozens of buildings were looted and destroyed, £5 million of damage was done and two Asian shopkeepers who kept the local sub-post office died.[17]

A report on the disturbances for the local council by the former MP Julius Silverman concluded that unemployment, deprivation and race discrimination were the causes of the riot.[18] Another report for the West Midlands county council was chaired by Herman Ouseley, assistant chief executive of Lambeth borough council. It also blamed deprivation. In addition it spoke of the 'day-to-day' oppression of the blacks and a bitter history of conflict between the local community and the police.[19] The local Labour MPs like Jeff Rooker had no more time for this nonsense than the Home Secretary, Douglas Hurd, who roundly condemned the riot as the work of 'criminal elements'. The police/community relations in this area had until then been quite good, which was one reason why the police were taken by surprise. The people who did regard the police as the enemy were local drug-dealers. They had begun with marketing cannabis but had moved over to selling heroin and cocaine in the street on a colossal scale and were frightened of the police cracking down. The riot was their response to police interference with their lucrative trade.[20] Needless to say the huge damage caused by the riot meant that the deprivation and unemployment from which the community suffered became palpably worse.

On 5 October 1985, during a raid on her home in Tottenham, Mrs Cynthia Jarrett, a respected figure in the local black community, was knocked over by a police officer and died of a heart attack despite efforts by the police to revive her. As a result the police were expecting trouble from resentful blacks from the enormous local housing estate, Broadwater Farm, but their guess was that it might take the form of a Brixton-style riot in the nearby shopping centre of Wood Green. Instead the police themselves were attacked on the Broadwater Estate. Attacks on police vehicles sent to pen the youths inside the estate soon turned into a full-scale clash of arms in which the police were at first heavily outnumbered and assailed by showers of missiles and petrol bombs. These were in such plentiful supply that many must have been prepared in advance. The situation was made worse by ambushes made easy by numerous overhead pathways on the estate. The police sustained heavy casualties and, in the worst incident of all, Police Constable Blakelock was hacked to death. According to one witness, the crowd surrounded him like vultures pecking at something on the ground. When his body was eventually recovered it bore forty stabs or cuts, and one six-inch gash in his cheek fractured and splintered the lower jaw.

The Metropolitan Police Commissioner later admitted that many technical mistakes had been committed in dealing with the riots. For instance the officers there were not trained to use plastic bullets. Yet the main fault was not technical but in the approach. The Broadwater Farm had become a textbook example of community policing and top priority had been given to forging links between people and police. But in practice, it had become a case of doing deals with bully boys and hardened criminals like Winston Silcotts, the man who played the leading role in the murder of PC Blakelock, for which he was tried and sent to gaol. As a result of this appeasement approach, according to a survey by three criminologists, half the women and one in seven of the men on the estate were frightened to go out after dark. In her scathing report written after the riot, Sergeant Gillian Meynell, who was in charge of the home-beat team, said she was ordered to brief her officers at the time of the Broadwater Farm festival in August 1985 to do nothing about the drugs they saw in order not to antagonize the black youths.[21] She also claimed that a week before the riot petrol bombs were being made and young blacks were having throwing practice. Despite police denials the estate had become, for a good deal of the time, a no-go area.

These two riots were moments of truth. Thereafter, the softly-softly policy made fashionable by the Scarman Report began to give ground to the traditional view: the enforcement of law and order must always come first.

7

Anti-Racism versus Freedom

In the demonology of the 'anti-racists' lobby blacks are poor and humiliated largely because of exploitation by whites. The cry of 'race equality' is therefore at least in part a demand for economic and social justice. It might be said that the anti-racist movement has applied a Marxist analysis of economics to the sphere of race relations, with whites in the role of capitalists and blacks as the working class. The parallel should warn us that simple appeals to our sense of justice, from 'anti-racists' as from Marxists, may mask sinister and subversive aims.

In practice the demand that the racial minorities shall have a juster distribution of status and rewards means replacing the free contractual arrangements between individuals by various forms of coercion by the state. When Communists took over a formerly free country they substituted the inequality of political and bureaucratic status — with all the control over the use of material resources that that implied – for simple inequality of wealth. Similarly many 'anti-racists' seek to impose a type of inequality which would give themselves more power, putting within their gift jobs, housing, special treatment by the welfare services, even the bestowing of qualifications through the grading of examinations and tests now controlled by others. The requirement that in almost every kind of transaction the ethnics must be fairly treated would result in the creation or enhancement in status of a huge number of posts of race controllers, supervisors, advisers investigators, assessors, arbitrators, prosecutors and judges, not to mention police. Clearly this would limit the freedom of the majority, and it is doubtful that there would be any compensating growth of freedom or even material gain for the ethnic minorities who are supposed to be the beneficiaries of such change. They may have special provision made for them where they had none before, but the price may be a new servitude to those who dispose of such privilege. All dependence means some freedom denied.

There is the subsidiary point that by being politicized ethnics may shy away from economically productive work. It may become easier to acquire an income or obtain a lucrative position through being on good terms with a politician or an official than to qualify for it by working hard This will both demoralize and impoverish people while also making them less independent. This argument is not academic. There are many parts of the world, including large parts of Africa and South America, where the social and political system is so debased that people who spend their days in useful toil are vastly worse off than those who constantly butter up, bribe and 'keep in with' corrupt politicians and officials. It is a social order which Professor Andreski has christened 'kleptocray'[1] or organized robbery which starts at the top. The outstanding characteristic of all countries run on this basis is that, however rich they may be in natural resources, their peoples are wretchedly poor.

The most obvious form which anti-racism regulation takes is interference with freedom of contract. A good example is the imposition of a statutory minimum wage which prevents the fixing of a wage below that figure even if it is voluntarily agreed between employer and employee. As has been mentioned in the chapter on American experience, in those states which imposed minimum wage rates the level of black youth unemployment jumped from being the same as for white youth to around twice as high. For the blacks who were thus put out of work the inability to take a job at a lower wage than the minimum rate was a real deprivation. The statutory minimum wage is likely to rob many Asian married women in Britain who do piece-work at home, where they are tied by custom and by young children, of what are sometimes described as 'starvation' wages, but which are still better than the alternative of nothing at all. Often these earnings are crucial in provid-ing the savings which create a family business and the in-dependence which goes with it. To introduce a minimum wage, as Britain's Labour government has done may seem like being on the side of the poorest, most downtrodden workers. Yet governments in South Africa intent on pre-serving apartheid deliberately used minimum wage laws to that end. Their aim was to reserve most jobs in certain occupations for whites. When they used quotas there was a temptation for employers to use more of the cheaper black labour than they were allowed. But after the imposition of minimum wage laws employers were reluctant to hire blacks at the same wage as whites.

Unions, again, are supposed to be the workers' champi-ons but they actually have a corporate monopoly interest in stopping the employment of workers below union rates. It is thus no coincidence that the Low Pay Unit, which constantly issues pamphlet deploring such practices as the use of sweated labour and has campaigned for the preser-vation of the wages councils (which impose wage minima on three million workers and which the Tories at one time threatened to abolish), is substantially dependent on trade unions for its funds. Not surprisingly the Labour party, which also receives most of its funds from trade unions, introduced a statutory minimum wage soon after gaining power in 1997.

It is true that the Labour party (like the Alliance) de-clares itself to be against racial discrimination in employ-ment and in favour of 'positive action'. It may thus be able to counter the detrimental effects to the ethnic minorities of a minimum wage. But imposing quotas or percentages of ethnic minority workers which organizations and firms must maintain nearly always involves lowering the standards which need to be achieved in order to qualify for a job. An unintended effect of this is to undermine the status of ethnics who qualify because people naturally assume that their qualification must be below par for the majority. Recently a black New York policeman refused to accept promotion to sergeant because, though he had passed the necessary examination and attained the marks required for ethnic minority candidates he had not reached the level demanded of the whites. He said he didn't want to be a 'quota sergeant'. He must have spoken for many self-respecting blacks who feel demeaned and their striving and achievements devalued by protection of this kind.

In many organizations the Commission for Racial Equality has found a back-door method of introducing what amount to ethnic quotas. Its method is to call on employers to monitor how many ethnic minority employees they have on their books. The proportion of ethnics to the total staff is then compared with the proportion of ethnics in the local population. If the ratio in the firm is lower the ethnics are said to be under-represented.

This is a deliberate confusion of equality of opportunity with equality of result. There is not the slightest reason to suppose that the lack of correspondence between the two percentages indicates racial discrimination; there are many other factors at work. All the same the CRE has managed to impose this *non sequitur* on all of government and local government bodies and hundreds of large private firms, including the clearing banks.[2]

The idea of imposing racial quotas was strongly advocated by John Carr in a Fabian pamphlet published in January 1987.[3] The form which this particular proposal took was the relatively new one of contract compliance. This is the policy of requiring those who receive public contracts to use a certain ratio of ethnic workers in carrying it out. It is copied from the USA where it is claimed that it has had a great success. Yet it is open to the same objections as a straightforward quota system, which, indirectly, is exactly what it is. Keeping up the ratio invariably involves lowering qualification standards, implying that ethnics are not sufficiently competent to pass at the same level as whites. It encourages us to ignore better solutions to the problem and is frequently harmful to the ethnics themselves.[4] It also implies large-scale resort to regulation at a time when governments are beginning to realize what damage to the economy regulations usually inflict.

A variant on the basic principle of positive action, though applied negatively, is the suspension from certain occupations or activities of people who are accused of racist conduct. Such is the effect of the Black List operated by the United Nations Special Committee Against Apartheid. Dozens of top British sporting personalities were excluded from competing in certain countries, including Nick Faldo, Harvey Smith and Sir Stanley Matthews. Their 'offence' was to take part in sporting events in South Africa, by which action thy are judged to support apartheid. Yet the underlying assumption of this measure — that anybody involved in South African sport was an accomplice in that country's racial policy — was surely questionable. The Thatcher government was in an equivocal position on sporting sanctions, having signed the Gleneagles Agreement by which it undertook to discourage sporting links with South Africa. Yet it consistently opposed other forms of sanction. Its other mistake was to have appointed a minister of sport, because this made politicians overseas assume that sport is a political matter in Britain — a collectivist idea with which Conservatives at least should have nothing to do. For it belongs to the totalitarian way of thinking according to which everything in human affairs lies within the province of politics. The civilized idea, which has taken such a beating in the past century, is that sport, like art, music, entertainment, religion, romantic love and family life, belongs to the civic culture which does not serve political ends.

The United Nations Black List extended to entertainment as well as sport, with more than 200 international show business personalities appearing on it. British stars on the list included Cliff Richard, Shirley Bassey and Spike Milligan.[5] Moreover, in April 1986 the British actors' union, Equity, voted to ban its members from visiting South Africa under pain of expulsion. This was not a penalty to take lightly because, in this tightly organized and unionized profession, the loss of their union card meant for most members the end of their career. The Equity ban came as a result of a postal ballot on a motion of the leftists in the union, in which just over 10 per cent took part and for which even so there was only a 58 per cent majority vote. Derek Bond, Equity president and former star of the West End farce, *No Sex Please, We're British*, resigned and Janet Suzman, a multi-prize-winning South African-born actress, was furious like many others at this gratuitous union interference with its members' affairs. She said, 'This ban is a lousy, stupid idea. No union has a right to dictate what a person's conscience should be. I abhor apartheid — but I also abhor political censorship. And politics should not come into any artistic profession.'[6] It was ironic that, in order to register a protest against (among other aspects of apartheid) the South African pass laws — which dictate where people may work and live — the activists of equity sought to impose pass laws on their own members. Happily a case was brought against the union and a High Court judge found that they were exceeding their authority — a true victory for civil liberty.

Yet more worrying than these attempts to influence people's behaviour by restricting their freedom to perform wherever they like, is the bid to win control of people's intellectual development. The anti-racist lobby fully realizes that the most effective way to impose its ideas on the population is to make them part of everybody's mental furniture. It can attempt to do this by building such ideas into the nation's education system, prescribing how it is to be organized and what is to be taught. This is what the Swann Report apparently set out to do. That report failed to answer the question of why West Indian children on average performed badly in school. The reason for that failure was that the committee made the fallacious assumption that equality of opportunity should mean equality of result. The inequality of West Indian academic performance could therefore only reflect unequal opportunities of which racialism must be the cause. Faced with a perceived failure of West Indians to adapt to British ways, as their poor school performance indicated, the Swann Report's prescription was that British society should be changed to accommodate West Indians, and other ethnic groups. This was to be done by conditioning the teachers in racial awareness courses and transforming the curriculum by placing far less emphasis upon English language and culture. The specific proposals which deserve attention (some were toned down in the final report but this is the general gist) were:

- An end to morning assembly with prayers;

- The teaching of ethnic group languages such as Gujarati, Punjabi and Creole even in all-white schools;

- The teaching of other subjects in these languages;

- The material taught in all subjects to be in accordance with the values of a multi-racial society and to the detriment of British patriotic pride;

- Ethnocentrism — in this case a European view of the world — to be expunged in the teaching of history and immigration to be presented as the legacy of the allegedly shameful episodes of empire and slavery.[7]

Such is the influence of the anti-racist establishment and its minions that this report, instead of being summarily rejected, was received seriously when it came out and many educational authorities, with the egregious Inner London Education to the fore, treated it as a *vade mecum*. Woe betide anyone in the education industry who dared to criticize the philosophy which it evidently distilled even before its final, as opposed to its interim, conclusions appeared. Yet one bold spirit, Ray Honeyford, headmaster of Drummond Middle School in Bradford, where 90 per cent of the pupils were Asian or black, did so dare in the winter of 1984. Writing in the obscure but academically eminent *Salisbury Review*, he accused the race lobby of exploiting the tolerance traditional in this country in order to induce and maintain feelings of guilt in the well-disposed majority, so that 'decent' people are 'not only afraid of voicing certain thoughts, they are uncertain even of their right to think those thoughts.' He criticized the dishonest terminology foisted on people by the race lobby. For instance there was the word 'racism' itself, which he called 'a slogan designed to suppress constructive thought ... the icon word of those committed to the race game.' He also objected to the perversion of the word 'black' to mean all non-whites with the obvious purpose of creating an atmosphere of anti-white solidarity. This was the preliminary before launching into specific complaints. He deplored the practice of many Asian parents of sending their children back to their homeland for a holiday during term-time to the detriment of their education. He objected strongly to the way they regarded freedom to do so contrary to law as a right. He also drew attention to the unrecognized plight of the white working-class children whose education was suffering in schools where they were hopelessly outnumbered by children from ethnic groups. He went on to reject the claim that West Indian educational failure owed anything to teacher prejudice or an alien curriculum and attributed it instead to 'West Indian family structure and values and the work of misguided radical teachers whose motives are basically political'. He finished by listing the various elements which were gathered together under the banner of multi-racialism and expressed his view that, far from producing harmony, they were operating to produce 'a sense of fragmentation and discord'.

These comments produced an explosion of wrath and mendacious propaganda from local activists of the race lobby who tried to have Mr Honeyford dismissed and, by constant abuse and picketing of the school, sought to make his life a misery. The Bradford Education Authority suspended him and though he was reinstated after a prolonged battle in the courts he eventually settled regretfully for early retirement, though on quite generous terms.

Jonathan Savery, who worked for the Local Education Authority in Avon which supported Mr Honeyford, also wrote in the *Salisbury Review*. As a result he was not only suspended by his employer but set upon by his colleagues. The National Union of Teachers, which had rightly shown itself anxious to defend Miss Maureen McGoldrick against Brent council's fabricated charges, instructed its members not to work with Mr Savery because he was a 'racist'. Which, as the *Salisbury Review* editorial was quick to observe, showed that merely to be charged with 'racism' nowadays is sufficient to be presumed guilty.

There is also some reason for thinking that the truth about events where a racial element is involved is being withheld. As was pointed out in Chapter Seven, the Metropolitan Police published figures in March 1983 on muggings in London which showed that over half of them were committed by blacks. Yet, though this information is of public interest, no more figures were produced after that date. Why? The short answer may be that, given the controversy over the figures caused by the race lobby, it is too troublesome to publish them. Such statistics are liable to complaints not only from the race relations quangos but from a militant clique in the National Union of Journalists. The NUJ code of conduct in clause 10 states: 'A journalist shall not originate material which encourages discrimination on grounds of race, colour, creed, gender or sexual orientation.' This for a start is objectionable because it is so ambiguous: no journalist can know for certain whether his or her material will encourage discrimination on grounds of race or any other of the grounds listed. Moreover the NUJ issues race relations guidelines urging members not to mention someone's race or nationality unless strictly relevant. On the face of it that sounds reasonable, but in any particular case judging what is relevant can be very difficult. The inevitable suspicion lurks that what we really have here is not a plea for fair play but for affirmative action on behalf of the racial minorities: they must always be given the benefit of the doubt. But the journalist has no business giving anybody the benefit of any doubt. His or her job is to report or establish the facts.

The guidelines also urge journalists to resist the temptation to sensationalize issues which could harm race relations. No one could object to the overt intention of that, but opinions vary about what constitutes sensationalism, and indeed about whether or not there are times and issues when sensationalism is justified. The pamphlet produced by NUJ activists in conjunction with the Campaign Against Racism in the Media, *It ain't Half Racist, Mum*, has an article by Carl Gardner which outlines a plan of action for fighting racism in the printed media. It starts mildly enough, suggesting, though without conviction, writing to the editor of the newspaper concerned. It goes on to recommend a series of escalations, complaining to the Press Council, raising the matter at a staff union meeting of the newspaper, drawing in the pressure groups and the other unions, calling a public meeting, and then proceeds to direct action, with picketing and occupation of newspaper offices to demand the right of reply. With the weakening of the unions since the Thatcher union reforms these bullyboy tactics became less effective.

Meanwhile the main 'anti-racist' pressure on newspapers has come from the Press Council, the body which was established to overlook the press in order to maintain standards. It is a necessary but unenviable job but the council made that job more difficult by impaling itself on the NUJ rubric that reports should not include 'irrelevant' references to race or colour. For all too often the charge of irrelevance appears to be no more than an attempt at censorship. For instance in 1985 all national newspapers reported the trial of a youth who raped five women and hacked another to death with a broken milk bottle. Several mentioned that the youth was black and were condemned by the Press Council because in its view the colour of the youth was not 'relevant'. The newspapers rightly castigated the Press Council's intervention as interference with editorial prerogative.

The race lobby has also made strenuous efforts to exert control over the reporting and commenting on racial matters on television. The Commission for Racial Equality produced a special report on 'Television in a Multi-Racial Society'.[8] This yielded a series of proposals — monitoring programmes, providing more jobs for ethnics as programme-makers and actors through positive action and so on. It reads as a programme for fair treatment — but stakes out a claim to power which if realized could result in television becoming subject to authoritarian controls.

In book publishing the 'anti-racists' have long been active. As early as 1972 an organization called 'Teachers Against Racism' wrote to the publisher of the famous children's classic *Little Black Sambo*, saying: 'the underlying message [of the book] is made all the more sinister by the appearance of innocence and charm. The reader swallows wholesale a totally patronizing attitude to black people who are shown as greedy [Black Sambo eats 169 pancakes], stereotyped, happy, clownish, irresponsible plantation "niggers".' This sort of pressure may well have had a cumulative effect as the book was later reported to be out of print.[9]

There are many more examples (others have been quoted in earlier chapters). The London borough of Brent figured prominently among them. In June 1982 it was reported that, following the appointment of an adviser on multi-cultural education there, Mrs Hettie Reith, headmistress of North View Primary School, Neasden, had been examining the books in the school library for material that was racially offensive. She lit upon *Dip the Puppy* by Spike Milligan, and wrote to him complaining, 'Your book shows a character "King Blackbottom" [described in the book as a big fat man in a grass skirt and a tin top hat] which in our opinion is an example of racial stereotyping totally at variance with current attitudes.' Shortly after this complaint the Inner London Education Authority drew up a blacklist of books which were 'potentially dangerous to young minds'. It included *Dr Doolittle*, in part of which a black man is depicted as a big buffoon, and *Beau and the Beast*, in which the beast is brown. Enid Blyton was also banned for a story about a grandmother's attitude to a black family who moved in next door. One of Walter de la Mare's short stories about a black boy who took medicine to turn himself white was also considered very harmful.[10]

Back in 1978 the veteran *Times* columnist Bernard Levin revealed anti-racist feeling among librarians, normally the most civilized and genteel of folk. He found a letter in the journal *Assistant Librarian* which declared not only that librarians had a duty 'to censor all material which is racist' but called for 'violent opposition' to stop racists voicing their views in the streets. He also unearthed an organization called 'Librarians for Social Change'. One of their manifestoes pronounced: 'LFSC is a forum for the reappraisal of getting information to the people. Our members are active in fighting the isms — capitalism, fascism, racism, sexism' — but not, apparently, Communism. Yet another organization called 'Librarians against Racism and Fascism' made the following ringing declaration:

> We, as library workers, agree that it is a major function of librarianship actively to combat racism and fascism and we advocate the following: that stock selection for libraries should be guided by anti-racist and anti-fascist principles. That staff recruitment should reflect a similar policy. That local authority buildings should not be used for racist or fascist organizations.[11]

Since then there have been several cases of these reference-room activists practising what they preach. The chief librarian of the London borough of Lambeth refused to obtain for one citizen a book on the British empire, *Noon Day Sun* by Valerie Pakenham, actually an amusing and mildly satirical book on the doings amid palm and pine of the Edwardian upper classes. His objection was that it was imperialistic and did not reflect the views of the coloured South African people. Predictably Lambeth also banned *Little Black Sambo* and *Uncle Tom's Cabin*.[12]

The ideologues of the race lobby, then, are capable of exerting limited control over people's lives in many different ways. While the Tories remained in office, however, their extremer tendencies were subject to some measure of restraint. The opposition parties, though, became committed to a forward policy on race, the details of which were apparently dictated by 'experts' supplied by the race lobby. That would surely mean accepting the CRE's proposals, already referred to, for augmenting its own powers under the 1976 Race Relations Act. Such an extension of its authority need not matter so much if it is merely an attempt to appropriate the already marked-out territory of a rival bureaucracy of quangocracy. Unfortunately it implies the acquisition by the CRE of alarming new inquisitorial and prosecutorial powers over the whole British population. Its proposals seek to enshrine in statute the fallacy according to which inequality of opportunity is proved by inequality of results. It wants to make the mere existence of 'unrepresentative' ratios of ethnic employment in any organization an automatic infraction of the law. Failure to fulfil racial quotas, which it would itself define, would become grounds for prosecution and, contrary to the whole tradition of British law, the onus of proof of innocence would rest upon the accused. And this greatly strengthened race relations law would apply far more comprehensively than it does today; for it would be given overriding priority, a great many present exemptions being elbowed out. The CRE aspires to control immigration and 'all areas of governmental and regulatory activity' including planning control, the prisons and the police. It could also, regardless of what the Secretary of State for Education might feel, interfere in the administration of schools.

Most ominously, under the proposed new regime race relations law would be shifted out of the ordinary courts and put under a new quango within the general framework of the industrial tribunal system. This body would be able to require the payment by offenders of large and, as far as employment matters were concerned, unlimited compensation to 'victims'.

On top of that the CRE would have unrestrained powers to impose codes of conduct on any organization with regard not only to employment but to any field of human relations. Again, where employment or housing benefit was concerned it would be able with the agreement of the Secretary of State for Employment to prescribe the keeping of ethnic records and the making of returns.

Under these proposals, the powers of the CRE to investigate and prosecute would resemble those of the Spanish Inquisition. Like Marx when he wrote the Communist manifesto, the Commission for Racial Equality scorns to conceal its intentions and no one can say that it has failed to give fair warning of what it is trying to achieve. It is entirely fitted to be the champion of the race lobby because it is so representative of so much of it, both in its hostility to our free institutions and in its urge to dismantle them in pursuit of its goal.

8

The Upside

I have argued in the preceding pages that racism is less of a problem in Britain than the extravagant response to it known as anti-racism, which has become a veritable mania. An industry of race inspectors, advisers and specialists has insinuated itself into every part of our national life. Where they have had power, as in some of our schools, they have used it dictatorially, as the persecution of Ray Honeyford in Bradford and many others less publicized has shown. This network of officials (most of them on the public payroll, but also making inroads in the private sector), has, far from furthering racial harmony which is supposed to be its purpose, fostered resentment and promoted strife.

Inevitably the race relations industry attracts some people who regard racial conflict as a means by which this country's democratic institutions may be undermined. For them the ethnic minorities are pawns in a class war whose divisions are drawn by race.

Yet the offensive against racism could not be sustained did it not touch deep chords in the national psyche relating to traumatic episodes in Britain's past. The word 'racism' arouses strong feelings because it evokes thoughts of Hitler, the British Empire and immigration. A combination of horror and misplaced sense of guilt shaped the liberal approach to racial issues in the post-war period. As a result it was easy for the anti-racist lobby to establish itself and become dominant in British life.

So it is that we are still contending with the quango legacy of politicians of 'liberal' cast of mind, the most conspicuous of whom was Roy Jenkins, Home Secretary in the critical mid-sixties and high priest of political correctness. His view — that immigration was good for Britain and that the majority should be socially engineered into accepting it — dictated our race relations legislation. It is he who was primarily responsible for the shift of emphasis from a limited semi-judicial function, dealing with acts of overt racial discrimination in public places and incitement to racial hatred, into active widespread harassment of organizations and individuals and the spreading of activist propaganda.

It did not take long for what eventually became the Commission for Racial Equality to follow the familiar path of regulative quangos and get taken over by a pressure group, in this case to become a mouthpiece of the ethnic groups. This partisanship of course conflicted with the CRE's judicial role. In any case the results of Jenkins's innovations were not happy in either sphere. Court cases bringing ordinary people to the dock over advertisements for Scottish cooks, Italian singers and European girlfriends, made the board, as it then was, a laughing-stock. There were many complaints about firms being investigated and arraigned to no good purpose and at great expense. The propaganda directed at the ethnic groups was even worse, being generally negative and inclined to encourage a dependency and a readiness to excuse every failing by blaming it on racial bias. Yet despite its poor results and signal lack of ordinary competence, which was underlined by a House of Commons Select Committee in 1981, the CRE harbours extraordinary ambitions for the extension of its role. It seeks ever more powers to enforce, throughout the length and breadth of the economy, policies of reverse discrimination or affirmative action which would create a bureaucratic nightmare and put valued traditional freedoms under threat. But these policies have already been tried and found wanting in the United States. The anti-poverty

programme of President Lyndon Johnson and his successors proved disastrous. At a cost so huge that it undermined
the standing of the American dollar it succeeded only in
making the situation of the poor blacks worse. This criticism has been eloquently voiced by a number of distinguished black academics of various disciplines. In CRE
circles, though, indeed in the race relations industry as a
whole, they and economists such as Thomas Sowell seem
to be either unknown or wilfully ignored. Nor do the CRE
bureaucrats seem to be aware of Charles Murray's path-
breaking *Losing Ground* which shows up the fundamental
defects of the anti-poverty programme: its stress on rights
instead of duties, its emphasis on state (federal) assistance
instead of neighbourhood help and the paternalism which
robs the poor of freedom and dignity of choice.

The spectacular riots of 1981 in Brixton, Birmingham
and Liverpool led to the official enquiry by the liberal-
minded Lord Scarman. In essence it traced the disturbances
to two common causes — police brutality and deprivation.
The recommendations led to the adoption of a softly-softly
approach to policing in racially-sensitive areas. The diagnosis was flawed and its prescription counter-productive.
Many of the police felt that it led ineluctably to the failure
at an early stage to control the 1985 Tottenham riot in which
PC Blakelock was killed.

Certainly the soft-softly policy did not stimulate any
corresponding softening on the part of the race-lobby
activists who in this period seemed more eager than ever
to vilify the police. The Scarman Report became a standard
progressive text, less for its philosophy of policing than
for its pronouncement that the riots were caused by
underlying social conditions such as joblessness, bad
housing and poverty's inevitable toll. The standard
progressive answer to this problem was to increase public
spending in these areas. Yet there had to be doubts about

such a solution if only because the riot areas had received more than most in the form of government grants. Moreover, the evidence did not support the contention that the ethnics were a deprived under-class. In particular the Asians who constituted half the ethnic population were in many respects, such as house ownership, educational achievement and business enterprise doing remarkable well. The core of the inner-city problem, in so far as it was an ethnic one was that of the West Indians. They suffered more from planning and municipal socialism than other inner-city dwellers because of their weak family structure, which was notable for the disproportionate number of one-parent, meaning in practice fatherless, families.

In many of Britain's inner cities comprehensive development planning has bought out and removed the small businesses and property-owners. This has not only destroyed a great many jobs but taken away such areas' natural leaders, leaving behind communities lacking in internal discipline easy prey to crime, vandalism and drugs. Municipal socialism, with its high rates drove away yet more businesses large and small, and encouraged the building of monster high-rise blocks of flats which are breeding grounds of social disorder and crime. All that the race relations industry and the left have to offer the West Indians caught in this trap are aggressive cultural chauvinism and welfare dependency which will inevitably make their conditions worse.

Those who persuade the ethnic communities that racial discrimination is the source of their ills and that politics is the cure are misleading them. As Lord Scarman said, there is no institutional racism in Britain and, unlike the American blacks, our ethnic minorities do not have to campaign for civil rights which they have long enjoyed. Politicians who offer to improve their condition by passing laws to end discrimination are in fact advocating special treatment.

The terrible plight of the North American Indians, who probably have more government-provided racial privilege than any other racial minority group in the world, is a warning to our ethnics to beware of those who, like the Greeks, come bearing gifts.

The good news is that neither the blacks nor the other ethnic minorities seem attracted to the communal approach to politics, but are swayed in their voting by national issues like unemployment rather than specifically ethnic issues such as racial discrimination. That is a good sign because Britain's blacks will prosper if they absorb themselves, as other ethnic groups have done, into the mainstream of British national life.

The laws and policies advocated by the race lobby to combat racism would not only do nothing to improve the material condition of the ethnic minorities but would also gravely infringe the traditional liberties of one and all. The harassment of numerous teachers and headmasters by left-wing local authorities is a pointer to the kind of tyranny that would be practised on a much larger scale. Even under the government of Mrs Thatcher the censoring influence of the race lobby on newspapers and the media through the Press Council, the TV and Radio Broadcasting Council and the activists of the National Union of Journalists was worrying, as was the censoring at local level of books and nursery rhymes.

It would not of course be practical to legislate against such perverse anti-racism, but there is certainly no reason to go on allowing public funds to sustain it. On the contrary, much would be gained by dismantling its infrastructure. It would be tempting from this point of view to abolish the Commission for Racial Equality altogether as well as the race relations legislation through which it came to be. Yet on balance there is a better case for reverting to the modest ambitions of the 1965 Act. These were to prevent incitement to racial hatred by making it a criminal offence, and to shield ethnic minorities against wounding overt acts of discrimination in public places. Incitement is a straight-forward matter which should be dealt with by the police. Discrimination in public places should where necessary be dealt with by injunction obtained by the Attorney-General, but preferably through the conciliation of the (as it then was) Race Relations Board. Admittedly this arrangement would leave *in situ* a band of race relations officers intent on exposing contraventions of the law. Yet it does address the problem of real racist behaviour which creates greater race tensions, generates ill-will among racial minorities and may lead to breaches of the peace. All the rest of the CRE apparatus, including its investigative, informative and propagandist functions should disappear.

Repealing the 1968 legislation, then, would not only dispense with most of the general staff of the race relations army but would also drastically reduce the race relations personnel in many private organizations and firms. Admittedly, at the local government level, where most of the race relations officers would not be needed either, they would probably be retained on ideological grounds. However, their influence should be limited by the change in the law. Where legislation fails to reduce extravagance and bad management the reform of local taxes to create an incentive towards economy in local government should be for the better; extraneous posts like those of race relations officers appointed to enforce legislation which has been repealed should be cancelled.

But how will the ethnic minorities fare under these arrangements? Few doubt that the Asians will flourish. They have become kings of the corner shop; indeed they probably saved the corner shop from extinction jut as it came under the supermarkets' competitive threat. Godfrey Smith, writing in *The Sunday Times*,[1] referred to Maheed

Mohammed, a Kashmiri Muslim, who would certainly welcome such changes. He complained that Brent council was forcing him to shut his supermarket next to Willesden tube station at 8.00 p.m. instead of midnight as was his wont, forcing him to work ninety hours a week instead of 110. As Smith observed, 'The Asians have found, with astonishing ease, yawning gaps in the British economy where it looks almost laughably easy to make money — provided you work hard enough and long enough.'

There are hundreds of Asian millionaires (of whom 100 or more are called Patel). The Durbar Club of Asian businessmen, referred to earlier, which supports the Conservative party, has a very high subscription. Most of its members have prospered not only through their own hard work, but because their whole family works as well; they don't take wages, so minimum wage laws don't affect them, and they plough their profits back into the business. It is characteristic of the anti-business psychology of many of our academics that a study of four Liverpool Polytechnic lecturers of Asian shops in 1982 decided that they were doomed. It concluded that their system, requiring long anti-social hours of work from the owner and substantial unpaid work from his family, was a waste of capital, talent and energy. The Asian shopkeepers remind one of the bee which the scientists, on the basis of aerodynamic theory, proved could not fly. The bee, unburdened by any knowledge of aerodynamics, just carries on flying.

But what about the West Indians? Certainly they have been conspicuously successful in sport. The Afro-Caribbean contribution to British sport is now phenomenal. They dominate boxing. A high proportion of players in professional football are black. The skill of West Indian cricketers is legendary. Certainly in sport the test — winning a race, or jumping higher or further than others or scoring more goals — is objective and race prejudice cannot affect the outcome. Yet perhaps it is more significant that sport is an area of life where the Afro-Caribbeans have confidence that they can win. Role models like Daley Thompson and Tessa Sanderson have bred a host of imitators among black youth, all reaching for the stars. Back performers have provided heroes for whites too and this has done more to counter racial prejudice than anything the race relations lobby has ever done. Typically the CRE has tended to ignore black success in sport and has drawn attention to occasions when crowds boo black players in order to show that race prejudice is on the increase. Yet it is a matter of record that in the USA black athletic prowess did more than anything else to breach the racial barriers in the universities of the Deep South. Nationally the brilliance of black players at baseball and basketball has done infinitely more for racial integration than any number of laws.

The justified hope is that the confidence engendered by black success in sport is spilling over into other areas of life. The effort and self-discipline through which Daley Thompson became the world decathlon champion would take a man to the top in any walk of life. He himself said, 'Even though all the other kids in school were white I never sensed I was different at all.' He believes that blackness is only an obstacle if it is allowed to be. 'If I went for a job where two A-levels were needed and a white guy with one A-level got the job, then I'd go away and get a university degree, then go back for the same job . . . I wouldn't even allow myself to think that colour had entered into it.'[2]

The Afro-Caribbeans do not have the merchanting tradition of the Asians or the kinds of families which work together as a unit without any individual wages. Yet something is moving. As mentioned earlier, West Indians are more motivated than the majority of whites and stay at school longer. When John MacGregor was industry minister he heard that West Indians had difficulties setting up their own businesses. So he organized a conference for Afro-Caribbean entrepreneurs, expecting about thirty to turn up. Judge his surprise when he found the meeting packed out with 150. It is a curious thing that, as *Guardian* reporter Leslie Goffe discovered,[3] West Indians from Britain who have gone to the United States are doing well in business. This suggests very strongly that there is no barrier to economic advance within West Indian culture but that there is some psychological factor peculiar to the situation in Britain which is holding them back. The Asian experience would suggest that this factor is not racism. My own view is that Britain's blacks have a huge potential for their own success and for the contribution they can make to national life. The principal reason why they have so far fallen short of fulfilling it is because they have been overexposed to the combined forces of the race lobby and the left, making excuses in anticipation of their economic failure before they have even begun to try. They have been targeted with the propaganda of those who for their own purposes want Britain's blacks to regard themselves as underdogs and to believe that the 'system', meaning competitive capitalism, is against them. There are indications that the new generation of black British are seeing through all that. They have a future full of promise if they recognize one thing: precisely because it is colour-blind, the free market is their friend.

Index

Notes

2 A Phobia for Our Time

1. *Anti-Racism, an Assault on Education and Value*, ed. Frank Palmer, Sherwood Press, 1986.
2. Ibid.
3. Ibid.
4. A reference to Peter Newsam, Chairman of the Commission for Racial Equality.

3 The Roots of Anti-Racism

1. *It ain't Half Racist, Mum*, ed. Phil Cohen and Carl Gardner Comedia Publishing, 1982.
2. *English History 1914-1945*, A.J.P. Taylor, Oxford University Press, 1965
3. *Why Six Million Died*, Arthur D. Morse, Seeker & Warburg, 1968.
4. *Anti-Racism*, op. cit.
5. *The Rise and Fall of the Third Reich*, William L. Shirer, Seeker & Warburg,
6. *Prelude to Genocide*, Simon Taylor, Duckworth, 1985.
7. *Anti-Racism*, op. cit.
8. *History of the Modern World*, Paul Johnson, Weidenfeld & Nicolson 1983-and, for the Stalin era, *The Great Terror*, Robert Conquest, Macmillan, 1968'
9. *This War Called Peace*, Brian Crozier, Drew Middleton and Jeremy Murray Brown, Sherwood Press, 1984.
10. *Spectator*, 7 February 1987.
11. *The Nation-Killers*, Robert Conquest, Sphere Books, 1972.
12. *The Economics and Politics of Race*, Thomas Sowell, William Morrow & Co., 1982.

13. *Markets and Minorities*, Thomas Sowell, Basil Blackwell, 1981.
14. *Reality and Rhetoric*, P.T. Bauer, Weidenfeld & Nicolson, 1984.
15. *The Irish in Britain*, Kevin O'Connor, Sigwick & Jackson, 1972.
16. *Race and Politics*, Mohammed Anwar, Tavistock Publications, 1986.
17. *Immigration and Race in British Politics*, Paul Foot, Penguin, 1965.
18. *Colour and Citizenship*, the Institute of Race Relations, Oxford University Press, 1969
19. *Freedom and Reality*, Enoch Powell, Batsford, 1969.

4 The CRE and Affirmative Action

1. *Race and Law*, Anthony Lester and Geoffrey Bindman, Penguin, 1972
2. *Roy Jenkins*, John Campbell, Weidenfeld & Nicolson, 1983.
3. *The Castle Diaries 1964-70*, Barbara Castle, Weidenfeld & Nicolson 1984
4. Hansard, 16 November 1961
5. *Towards Tomorrow*, Fenner Brockway, Hart-Davis, MacGibbon 1977
6. *Daily Telegraph*, 27 October 1969.
7. *The Times*, 25 November 1969 and *Daily Telegraph* 17 December 1969
8. *Daily Mail*, 21 November 1969.
9. Ibid., 1 November 1969.
10. Ibid., 5 May 1970.
11. *Daily Telegraph*, 13 April 1970.
12. *Daily Mail*, 31 January 1970.
13. *The Times*, 19 February 1970.
14. *Daily Mail*, 20 January 1971.

15. Ibid., 26 March 1971.
16. *The Awkward Warrior*, Geoffrey Goodman, Davis-Poynte, 1979.
17. *Freedom and Reality*, op. cit.
18. *Against Equality*, ed. William Letwin, Macmillan, 1983.
19. 'Against Equality Again', J.R. Lucas, *Against Equality*, op. cit.
20. 'Race and Affirmative Action', John Bowers and Suzanne Franks, Fabian Tract 471, 1980.
21. *Daily Mail*, 24 October 1983.
22. Ibid., 28 August 1978.
23. *Daily Telegraph*, 30 July 1986.
24. *Daily Mail*, 30 July 1982.
25. *The Times*, 18 June 1982.
26. *Sunday Telegraph*, 6 December 1981.
27. *Daily Telegraph*, 5 May 1982.
28. *The Times*, 15 October 1980.
29. 'Immigration Control Procedures', a summary of the CRE report produced by the National Association of Community Relations Councils, 1985.
30. 'Loading the Law', Alan Little and Diana Robins, Commission for Racial Equality, July 1982.
31. 'Employment Prospects for Chinese Youth in Britain', Alfred Chan, Commission for Racial Equality, July 1986.
32. *Daily Telegraph*, 15 August 1982.
33. *Daily Mail*, 6 October 1981.
34. 'Report on the Seminar on Racism Awareness Training', Commission for Racial Equality, October 1984.
35. 'Housing Need Among Ethnic Minorities', Commission for Racial Equality, December 1977.
36. 'Racial Equality and Social Policies in London', Commission for Racial Equality, August 1980.
37. 'Racial Equality and the Youth Training Scheme',

Commission for Racial Equality, October 1984.

38. First Report of the Home Affairs Committee, HMSO, 1981.
39. *Daily Telegraph*, 21 September 1976.
40. Ibid., 10 September 1983.
41. *Guardian*, 7 March 1984.
42. CRE Annual Report, 1985; see Appendix 5.

5 American Lessons We Don't' Learn

1. The Scarman Report, Lord Scarman, Pelican Books 1982
2. *Economic Affairs*, December/January 1986/7
3. The New Black Intellectual', Murray Friedman, Commentary, June 1980
4. *America: A Minority Viewpoint*, Walter E. Williams, Hoover institute Press,
5. Policy Review, July 1978.
6. See in particular the following three books by Sowell: *Race and Economics*, Longmans, 1975; *Markets and Minorities*, Blackwell, 1981; *The Economics of Politics and Race*, William Morrow & Co., 1983.
7. *America's Apartheid*, National Review, 8 May 1987.
8. *Markets and Minorities*, op. cit.
9. *Losing Ground*, Charles Murray, Basic Books 1984
10. *The Triumph of Politics*, David Stockman, the Bodley Head 1986
11. 'A Conservative Vision of Welfare', Stuart M. Butler, *Policy Review*, Spring 1987.
12. 'Who Speaks for American Blacks', Glenn C. Lowry, Commentary, January 1986.

6 Scarman and the Riots

1. CRE Annual Report, 1985.

2.   *Daily Telegraph*, 28 July 1981.
3.   *Daily Mail*, 13 April 1981.
4.   Ibid, 11 July 1981.
5.   *Daily Telegraph*, 28 July 1981.
6.   *Commentary*, September 1977.
7.   *Economist*, 18 July 1981.
8.   *Daily Mail*, 13 July 1981.
9.   *Sunday Telegraph*, 27 May 1984.
10. *The Times*, 10 September 1984
11. Ibid., 25 July 1986.
12. *Guardian*, 20 October 1984.
13. *Daily Telegraph*, 30 October 1984.
14. *Daily Express*, 8 October 1985.
15. *Daily Mail*, 28 July 1982.
16. *Daily Mail,* 8 October 1985.
17. *Daily Mail*, 11 September 1985.
18. Ibid., 28 February 1986.
19. Ibid., 21 February 1986.
20. Ibid., 15 September 1985.
21. Ibid., 21 January 1986.

7 Anti-Racism versus Freedom

1.   *Parasitism and Subversion: the South American Case*,
     Stanislav Andreski Weidenfeld & Nicolson, 1966.
2.   CRE Annual Report, 1985.
3.   'Contract Compliance for the UK', John Carr, Fabian
     Society, January 1987.
4.   *America: A Minority Viewpoint*, Walter Williams,
     Hoover Institution Novem-ber 1982.
5.   *Daily Mail*, 27 October 1983.
6.   Ibid., 12 April 1986.
7.   'The Wayward Curriculum', ed. Dennis O'Keefe, So-
     cial Affairs Unit, 1986.
8.   'Television in a Multi-racial Society', Muhammad

Anwar and Anthony Shang, Commission for Racial Equality, 1984.

9. *Daily Telegraph*, 5 October 1985.
10. *Week End*, 18 January 1984.
11. *The Times*, 30 May 1978.
12. *Daily Express*, 27 September 1985.

8 The Upside

1. *The Sunday Times*, 26 February 1984.
2. *Daily Mail*, 31 December 1982.
3. *Guardian*, 11 June 1986.

Postscript

Discouraging

Since completing the final draft of this new edition, there
have been important, if   mostly disheartening developments in race relations in Britain. As indicated above, my
belief is that immigration into this country, if properly
managed, in terms of numbers allowed in and the quality
of the intake, should prove to be a net benefit in the long
term as it has been in America, which, after all is a nation
of immigrants. Even well-managed immigration however
can create hardship for some of the original inhabitants,
especially the poor and unskilled, in terms of jobs, housing, education and services. Moreover, even a sound immigration policy can have negative results if it is not associated with other policies directed at integrating the
immigrants into the community. Sadly, current prospects
are discouraging on both counts. I say this with regret because the present Home Secretary, David Blunkett, a huge
improvement on his predecessor Jack Straw, appears, at
least from his public pronouncements, to be making a genuine to attempt to face up to some of the real problems. He
has been prepared to brave the wrath of the race relations
lobby in speaking of "swamping " — he was thinking only
of certain schools and medical practices being overwhelmed
by asylum seekers needing interpreters and special services. But what a racket there was when Margaret Thatcher
dared to use the same word! (*Times* 28.04.02). He has also
been bold enough to criticise Asian arranged marriages with
spouses from the Indian sub-continent — and with reason,
because the introduction of spouses with little knowledge
of English tends to prolong the ghettoisation of many of
the Asian community. Blunkett's approach, outlined in a

white paper, (*Times* 8.2.02) provides for tests in English
and UK culture for applicants; a revised citizenship pledge
and ceremonies for new citizens; an expansion of schemes
allowing youngsters to enter the UK to work; the creation
of four accommodation units of 3000 asylum applicants;
and the stripping of citizenship from suspected war criminals and terrorists. Yet the formidable scale of the numbers
problem is shown by the fact that fewer than 20,000 failed
asylum-seekers have been ejected over the last two years
out of 150,000 applicants who have been refused. (*Daily
Telegraph* 1.3.02). It looks as if it will be a long time before this inflow, if ever, comes under control.

Fifth Column

Besides, there is a new cause for alarm about some of those
who have already made their homes here. Following
Britain's involvement in a full-scale war against the Taliban
government of Afghanistan, evidence has emerged that
many young British Moslems have identified with the
enemy, that indeed there is a numerous real or potential
fifth column in our midst. An opinion poll by an Asian
radio station, Sunrise, revealed that 98 per cent of Moslems
in London under the age of 45 would not fight for Britain
while 48 per cent said that they would take up arms for
Osama Bin Laden. Manzoor Moghal, chairman of the
Federation of Moslem Organisations in Leicester called
this "a terrible indictment of the policy of multiculturalism,
which has allowed extremism to flourish and which has
failed to generate any feelings of national allegiance among
some of our biggest ethnic minorities." He went on to blame
the Home Office not only for failing to clamp down on
anti-western fundamentalist clerics fostering hate but for
actually giving them welfare benefits and accommodation.
Urban local authorities were also at fault, he said, for

promoting segregation by handing out 'community grants' giving support to different racial groups in return for political support. The clear implication, he believes, is that Britain should learn from America and seek to inculcate in immigrants the common values and traditions of their new homeland. Yet, as he remarked, when Home Secretary David Blunkett suggested that immigrants should learn English and go to classes in British heritage, he was immediately accused of 'racism'. (*Daily Mail* 31.10.2001 Manzoor Moghal, "As a Moslem I say this multicultural nonsense has a lot to answer for").

Anti-Brits

The seriousness of the situation was underlined by the arrest of Richard Colvin Reid, a British man of Jamaican descent and a convert to Islam, when he attempted to set off a shoe-bomb on American Airlines Flight 63 between Paris to Miami. It turned out that he had been converted to Islam while in a British prison. According to Theodore Dalrymple, a prison doctor, who writes a regular column in the *Spectator*, there is nothing surprising about this conversion because our prisons are deluged with Islamic literature, far exceeding in quantity any material about Christianity. Also conversion to Islam is a way of expressing enmity to our society by those who have a grudge against it, while also releasing them from any sense of personal responsibility to it.

The Government's overriding concern in all this has been to stress again and again that it is not anti-Islam. While of course it is sensible not to play Osama Bin Laden's game and accept that the West is engaged in a conflict with Islam, Home Secretary David Blunkett went too far with proposals for a law against incitement to religious hatred, which, incidentally, has long been on the agenda of the

CRE. This would have created the absurdity of enforcing penalties against insults directed at Islam, or for that matter the Moonies, at a time when the laws against blasphemy against the Christian religion, though still extant, have been practically out of use since the nineteenth century. Happily Mr Blunkett's proposals failed to reach the statute book, but this episode showed the direction in which we could be heading.

More Coercion

Nonetheless, if there has been some improvement in the direction of asylum and immigration policy, as far as internal race relations are concerned the CRE and Macpherson-inspired bullying and hectoring approach is more pervasive and intrusive than ever. This has taken tangible form of compelling all of 40,000 public bodies, down to the Apple and Pear Research council and the Scottish Deer Commission, to follow a long detailed and legally-binding code of practice which puts race at the top of their priorities. A 255-page code of rules produced by the Commission for Racial Equality prescribes targets for 'positive action' by all the public services. The targets, mainly concerning the racial representativeness of staff, are of course quotas in all but name (*Daily Mail* 4.12.01). I said "all public bodies", but there is one scandalous exception, namely the CRE itself, the ruling body of which, the ten person Commission, contains only one non-ethnic. It is bizarre, to say the least, that this Commission, which has only 10 per cent of its membership to represent 94 per cent of the taxpayers which finance it, has been given the task of monitoring the ethnic targets of all other public bodies, and punishing those which do not conform. Who shall monitor the monitors? The point is important. If the majority of the community has only token representation on the CRE Commission, how are the members to think of themselves other than as apologists and delegates for the minorities? It is an extreme case of a government regulatory agency, supposedly neutral, being captured by the interest groups it is meant to supervise. Maybe it is because it senses that its own position is so anomalous that the CRE is so insistent that 'targets' do not mean quotas and that 'positive action' does not mean positive discrimination, though anyone who has not actually been brainwashed will see no difference. It is possible, of course, that those responsible for these new rules are merely trying to create confusion about the true position. No doubt they realized that positive discrimination in favour of ethnic groups was the tinderbox which ignited the serious riots in Bradford and neighbouring areas in July 2001. What is certain, though, is that these laws will decrease the efficiency of public services at the very time when their improvement is supposed to be at the forefront of the Government's concerns.

Stop and Search Stymied

The worrying thing is the way that what appear to be promising moves by government turn out to be additional bureaucratic burdens. Thus the decision of David Blunkett to resume stop and search activities by the police looked like a sudden rush of commonsense. However this new initiative was accompanied by the requirement that the police provide those they question on the streets with notes of the episode. Dr Marian Fitzgerald, who studied the use of stop-and-search powers for the Home Office, said that the idea of handing out records was "complete madness, a nonsense".

CRE Still Power-hungry

Not content with the big extension of its powers of coercion referred to above, the CRE, its satraps and toadies, are actively seeking to spread their tentacles still wider. Thus Sir David Calvert-Smith, the director of public prosecutions declared in June 2002 that almost all British people were institutionally racist. This may indeed have been mainly an exercise in self-defence because the Crown Prosecution Service was branded racist by two reports in 2001. Sir David was really saying that, if he and his organisation were racist, they were just the same as everyone else. (*Sunday Times* 23.6.02.) Perhaps he was taking his cue from the pronouncement a fortnight earlier of the diocesan Bishop of Birmingham Dr Sentamu, the only black member of the inquiry into the police investigation of Stephen Lawrence's death and the driving force behind the Macpherson Report. He accused the Church of England of institutional racism just at the juncture when the Crown Appointments Board was considering the merits of Dr Michael Nazir Ali, Bishop of Rochester, who was born in Pakistan, as a successor to Dr George Carey (*Times* 12.6.02).

Just how insidious such anti-racist campaigning can be was shown by the announcement by the Scottish executive of the policy on race which every Scottish school will have to introduce by 2004. It will include ways to improve the exam results of pupils from ethnic backgrounds! One wonders how many extra marks will be awarded to pupils for being black. Meanwhile, in another part of the government, its curriculum body has been having second thoughts and has reversed the politically correct anti-racist education of the past. Worried about the alienation of white pupils by its former concentration on ethnic culture, it has told teachers to instil in their pupils a "pride in white culture". (*Sunday Times* 3.2.02). This didn't stop delegates to the head Teachers Conference in Torquay demanding the following June that Punjabi and Gujarati should be studied instead of French and German (*Times* 7.6.02).

Since art is an imitation of life it was hardly to be expected that the acting profession should escape the attentions of the politically correct. Thus, after a damning report finding institutional racism among thespians, the Arts council decided to impose quotas for black and Asian actors, or what it called "non-negotiable targets"(*Times* 19.4.02).

This brief catalogue of folly would not be complete without reference to the parking questionnaire issued by the Royal Borough of Kensington and Chelsea, which included the question: "To which ethnic group do you consider you belong?" This prompted Sunday Times columnist Minette Marrin to ask "which racial sub-group would you like to park in?" (*Sunday Times* 2.6.02).

Little for our Comfort

In light of the above, the most hopeful forecast one can make about the future of race relations in Britain is that they will get worse before they get better. Fortunately, as can be judged from some of the preceding press reports and comments, a more sceptical attitude towards the shibboleths of the race relations industry has developed in the media, especially since the terrorist attack in New York on September 11th 2001. Even so, anti-racism remains the most virulent form of political correctness threatening freedoms of speech and opinion in Britain today. It is time for all good men and women to spring to their defence. The Latin-speaking Roman Empire provides a precedent. It was monocultural and multiethnic and it lasted for hundreds of years, despite serious misgovernment and repeated incursions by outsiders. A monocultural, multiethnic Britain is the way ahead.